FUN WITH DNA

RICK GEARY © 18

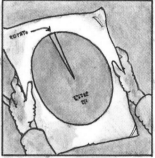

I WAS ALWAYS TOLD THAT OUR FAMILY HAILED FROM THE LAND OF SLOVENIA.

WE DANCED IN TRADITIONAL COSTUMES...

ENJOYED THE NATIONAL DISHES...

AND SANG THE MOURNFUL BALLADS OF THE OLD COUNTRY.

OUT OF CURIOSITY I BOUGHT ONE OF THOSE ANCESTRY KITS.

I SPIT INTO A TUBE AND SENT IT OFF TO A LAB IN CALIFORNIA.

TO MY SURPRISE, I FOUND THAT I'M ONLY 2% SLOVENIAN — AND 98% "OTHER."

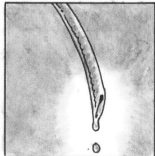

I CONTACTED THE LAB, BUT THEY WERE QUITE CURT AND EVASIVE.

AND SO I ASKED MY MOTHER, WHO MADE A STARTLING CONFESSION...

MANY YEARS AGO, A BRIGHT, PULSATING CRAFT APPEARED OUTSIDE HER WINDOW.

SHE WAS ABDUCTED BY ITS OCCUPANTS AND IMPREGNATED THRU A LONG NEEDLE.

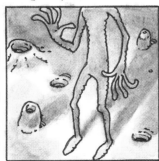

I'VE JUST RETURNED FROM A VISIT TO MY NEWFOUND FAMILY IN THE ALPHA CENTAURI SYSTEM.

NOW I KNOW WHERE MY WIRY PHYSIQUE COMES FROM...

AND MY WINSOME SMILE ...

NOT TO MENTION MY THIRST FOR HIGH ADVENTURE!

B

BY MICHAEL GERBER

BOLDLY GOING THERE

Voyages of the Starship Free Enterprise

*F*or over fifty years now, Star Trek *has been a wildly successful, quite reassuring vision of Humanity's future. But Roddenberry's show assumed that the liberal 1960s would set the tone for the centuries to come. After the last few years, it seems that the voyages of Captain Kirk and the rest could turn out very different...*

KIRK
(voice over)
Captain's Log, Stardate 6270 years after Genesis. I, James T. Kirk, Captain of the USS Free Enterprise, have undertaken a for-profit expedition to find breathable oxygen for the gated planet Aynrand 7. We had hoped to run a typical strong-arm operation on the pathetic star-hippies of the Copernicus Commune. We'd offer to pay them generously, then once they agreed to the deal and lowered their defenses, we'd appear in orbit with photon torpedoes aimed at their capital city. Then we'd siphon off their entire atmosphere—for free.

KIRK
(cont.)
Aim those torpedoes at the corner of Alinsky Street and Chomsky Boulevard, Mr. Sulu.

SULU
Aye aye, Captain. Locking photon torpedos...now.

MICHAEL GERBER

(@mgerber937) is Editor & Publisher of *The American Bystander*.

[*SFX: Revving engines, a small explosion, the "red alert" siren.*]

KIRK
Are we under attack? Scotty, what's going on?

SCOTT
Captain, we've had another malfunction. For some reason, pushing the torpedo button engaged the warp drive.

KIRK
Spare me the *science*, Mr. Scott. Give it to me in English, the official language of Starfleet.

SCOTT
The Free Enterprise is a piece of junk, Captain. She was built by the Emperor's idiot son Prince Jared XXIII. I'm surprised she's even airtight.

[*The RED ALERT siren expires, with a sickly wheeze.*]

SCOTT
See what I mean? Bloody grifters.

KIRK
I'll thank you to keep your socialism to yourself, Mr. Scott. Can you fix her?

SCOTT
Not without coal, Captain. Lots and lots of coal.

KIRK
Just keep us in orbit, Scotty. I'll get your coal...somehow. Kirk out. Lieutenant Uhura, I need you to send a coded tweet out on all channels. "This is James T. Kirk on the USS Free Enterprise. Don't believe fake news media that I'm stuck out here on a starship built by slave labor, orbiting some

shithole planet like a dog. Haters are in for a big surprise!" Capitalize words randomly, and misspell a few, to show that education is for losers.

UHURA
Aye-aye Captain.

KIRK
Biblical Officer Spock—what can you tell me about this rock? Is it inhabited?

SPOCK
Affirmative, Captain. The lifeforms appear to be sentient, bipedal and non-Christian.

KIRK
Excellent. Mr. Sulu, you've been through conversion therapy. You'll come with us, to convert the natives.

SULU
Uh, that's not the type of conversion I—

KIRK
(cutting SULU off)
Mr. Spock, is the atmosphere breathable? Can we steal it for Aynrand 7?

SPOCK
Affirmative, Captain.

KIRK
And what does the Good Book say about that?

SPOCK
Proverbs 12:24 comes to mind: "The hand of the diligent will rule, while the slothful will be put to forced labor."

KIRK
Good enough for me. Mr. Chekov, will

you take the conn while the rest of us go down and introduce these savages to capitalism?

CHEKOV
I am Russian, Captain. You can trust me.

KIRK
Good. Spock, you'll team with me. Sulu will go with—Uhura, would you like to come? I'll offer you 80 cents on the dollar.

UHURA
I'd love to, Captain.

KIRK
Good. There could be some cooking and/or cleaning to be done. Mr. Sulu, you look uncomfortable.

SULU
Captain, no offense to Uhura, but I can't be alone with a woman other than my wife.

KIRK
We wouldn't want to infringe your religious freedom. Uhura, forget it. We'll get McCoy.

SPOCK
I'm afraid he's in sickbay, Captain. There's been an outbreak of measles.

KIRK
Well, at least it's not autism. Come on.

[*TRANSITION MUSIC over shot of USS FREE ENTERPRISE, rounding a planet in orbit. If you look closely, you see STUFF FALLING OFF the ship.*]

KIRK
(*voice over*)
Captain's log, Stardate 6270.2. For once the USS Free Enterprise's transporters worked—but not without cost.

Accepting my challenge that "coordinates were for elitists," Mr. Scott used his gut, and transported Mr. Sulu into a slab of solid rock. But Spock, McCoy and I arrived safely on the planet...which is inhabited by one of the strangest lifeforms ever encountered.

"All right. I'll give you 130,000 credits, but not a word to the press."

We see KIRK, SPOCK and McCOY all crouched behind a very flimsy-looking boulder. They speak quietly, so as not to be heard by the aliens conversing ten feet away.

KIRK
Remarkable. One side of their faces is white, while the other is black. Literally "good people on both sides."

SPOCK
Indeed, Captain. The identity politics alone are mesmerizing.

Dr. McCoy is covered with red spots, which he scratches as he talks.

McCOY
(*irascibly*)
I guess blackface is okay on this planet. Whiteface, too.
(*beat*)
I wonder if they're good dancers on the left side of their bodies.

SPOCK
Ecclesiates 3:7, Doctor. "There is a time to keep silent, and a time to speak."

McCOY
You're just mad you're not the only half-breed.

ALIEN
Stay right where you are!

Our heroes look up to see an ALIEN standing behind them, his phaser-type gun trained directly on their heads. In his other hand, he holds a roll of duct tape — clearly a bad hombre.

ALIEN
(*cont.*)
Hands up!

KIRK
We are officers of the USS Free Enterprise. We come in peace, with a once-in-a-lifetime business opportunity.

ALIEN
Silence! You are all in "no-face," which will all find extremely offensive. For that, you must die!

[*DRAMATIC MUSIC STING, and we go to commercial.*] ◗

TABLE OF CONTENTS

JOHN CUNEO

The AMERICAN BYSTANDER

#10 • Vol. 3, No. 2 • March 2019

EDITOR & PUBLISHER
Michael Gerber
HEAD WRITER
Brian McConnachie
SENIOR EDITOR
Alan Goldberg
CONTACTEE Scott Marshall
ORACLE Steve Young
STAFF LIAR P.S. Mueller
INTREPID TRAVELER
Mike Reiss
**AGENTS OF THE SECOND
BYSTANDER INTERNATIONAL**
Craig Boreth, Matt Kowalick,
Neil Mitchell, Maxwell Ziegler
MANAGING EDITOR EMERITA
Jennifer Boylan
CONTRIBUTORS
Luke Adams, Ikenna Azuike, Penny Barr,
Charles Barsotti, Alex Bernstein, George
Booth, Dylan Brody, M.K. Brown, Adam
Chase, David Chelsea, Dave Croatto,
John Cuneo, Ivan Ehlers, Meg Favreau,
Emily Flake, Drew Friedman, James Finn
Gardner, Lucas Gardner, Rick Geary,
Sam Gross, Lance Hansen, Ron Hauge,
Khadjiah Johnson, Victor Juhasz, Lars
Kenseth, Riane Konc, Ken Krimstein,
Stephen Kroninger, Jeffrey Kulik, Peter
Kuper, Rob Kutner, Sara Lautman, Ross
MacDonald, Stan Mack, Merrill Markoe,
James McMullan, Mia Mercado, Jeremy
Nguyen, Joe Oesterle, Michael Pershan,
Jonathan Plotkin, Denise Reiss, Peter Sa-
lomone, Cris Shapan, Mike Shiell, Rich
Sparks, Nick Spooner, Ed Subitzky, Tom
Toro, D. Watson.
THANKS TO
Kate Powers, Rae Barsotti, Lanky Ba-
reikis, Jon Schwarz, Alleen Schultz, Molly
Bernstein, Joe Lopez, Eliot Ivanhoe, Neil
Gumenick, Mary McCullough, Thomas
Simon, Greg and Patricia Gerber and
many, many others.
NAMEPLATES BY
Mark Simonson
ISSUE CREATED BY
Michael Gerber

The TANGENTS TALK IT OVER

@MK Brown

END

CARTOONS & ILLUSTRATIONS BY
A. Birch, J. Cuneo, D. Fefee, S. Gross, R. Hauge, C. Hankin, N. Jones, V. Juhasz, J. Krossner, P. Kuper, J. Nguyen, D. Watson.

COVER

Our covers are my special delight, and never more than this one by the marvelous **JAMES McMULLAN**. It beautifully epitomizes our ongoing national catastrophe; when I posted it on Facebook in late February, the reaction was immediate, and visceral. It reminds me of photos from June 1968, showing Americans of all types standing on grassy railway embankments, as Robert F. Kennedy's funeral train passed from New York to Arlington. Jim once said, "There's a kind of melancholy in all of my work." Perhaps that's what makes it particularly resonant in our current era. Thank you, Jim.

ACKNOWLEDGMENTS

All material is ©2019 its creators, all rights reserved; please do not reproduce or distribute it without written consent of the creators and *The American Bystander*. The following material has previously appeared, and is reprinted here with permission of the author(s): Stan Mack's "The Science of Love" first appeared in *The Village Voice*. Richard Littler's Brexit poster on page 27 can be purchased by going to the Saatchi Gallery store: https://bit.ly/2Obuk9v.

---◆---

THE AMERICAN BYSTANDER, *Vol. 3, No. 2*, (978-0-578-48397-9). Publishes ~4x/year. ©2019 by Good Cheer LLC. No part of this magazine can be reproduced, in whole or in part, by any means, without the written permission of the Publisher. For this and other queries, email *Publisher@ americanbystander.org*, or write: Michael Gerber, Publisher, *The American Bystander*, 1122 Sixth St., #403, Santa Monica, CA 90403. **Subscribe at www.patreon.com/bystander.** Other info can be found at www.americanbystander.org.

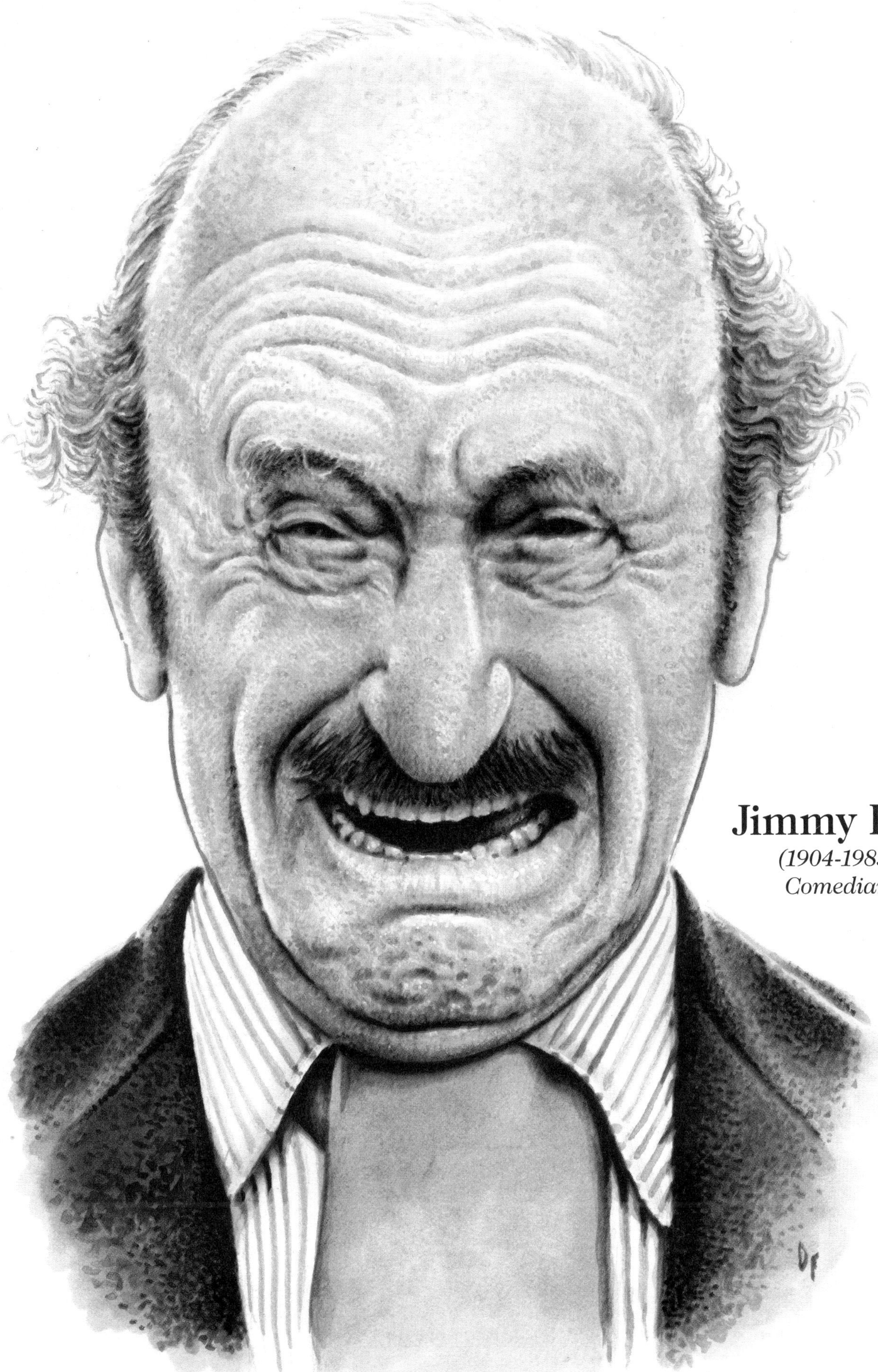

Jimmy Ritz

(1904-1985)
Comedian

NEWS & NOTES

A talk at Parsons! Movies! Books! References that were old when Hector was a pup!

Ten issues! Break out the hats and hooters! In the words of the Greek poet Pindar, "Who woulda thunk it?" Before we lose ourselves in revelry, however, I'd like to extend a great big hope-your-credit-card-processes-properly welcome to all our new subscribers. I know you've been looking for jokes referencing Pindar and Steely Dan, we all have. Look no further: you're home.

America being a capitalist paradise and the literary arts being a crappy way to make a living, *Bystander* contributors are an *insanely* active lot. As a result, we are always trying to figure out how to keep readers appraised of their various doin's. Our latest scheme—a brainstorm of Marketing Maven Maxx Ziegler—is running a calendar on our Facebook page (*www.facebook.com/americanbystander*). Browse on over and see what you think; we'll add readings, presentations and talks as our contributors' supply them.

Case in point: yours truly has been invited by Parsons' **BEN KATCHOR** to lead a panel featuring **EMILY FLAKE**, **DREW FRIEDMAN**, **STEPHEN KRONINGER**, **SAM GROSS** and **STEVE YOUNG**. We'll be talking about humor magazines, nationally and internationally, and *Bystander*'s place in that thin crowd; It's happening at 7:00 p.m. on Tuesday, April 16, at Parsons' University Center, Room UL105, 63 Fifth Avenue, in New York City. All of you are heartily encouraged to attend. I'll bring lipstick and kiss everybody's issues (more personal than a signature, don't you think?).

Bystander **RISA MICKENBERG** has written a movie called *EGG*, which boasts a sparkling 100% on Rotten Tomatoes. Risa wrote to say that "it's streaming now on Amazon, iTunes, On Demand and on Vudu. (Whatever that is.)" It's the future, Risa. *The future.*

The aforementioned Steve Young is the subject of a documentary, *Bathtubs over Broadway*, still popping up in festivals across the country. When it's streamable, I'll let everybody know; until then, go to *www.bathtubsoverbroadway.com/screenings* to see if it's showing near you. I saw the film here in Santa Monica and loved it. Detailing Steve's unlikely obsession with industrial musicals, by the last reel *Bathtubs* becomes the most exu-

berant, heartfelt exhortation to follow one's dream since, well, *The Boys from Brazil*.

For those of you who prefer using your ears, **MERRILL MARKOE** and **MEGAN KOESTER** have produced an Audible audiobook for the ages, *The Indignities of Being a Woman*. I downloaded it last week and am loving it; you will, too, whatever your gender. I don't think I'll be giving too much away if I quote Merrill: "The bullshit begins around 3,000 B.C."

They called James Brown "the hardest working man in show business," but compared to **BOB ECKSTEIN**, J.B. was a piker. Bob's got a new collection out: *The Ultimate Cartoon Book of Book Cartoons*. This recursively titled compendium features contributions from a whole shelffull of Bystanders, including **GEORGE BOOTH**, **MICK STEVENS**, **SAM GROSS**, **ROZ CHAST**, **JACK ZIEGLER**, **LIZA DONNELLY**, **P.C. VEY**, **NICK DOWNES** and **SIDNEY HARRIS**. Fans of books, cartoons, books with cartoons, or cartoons about books will *not* be disappointed.

MORT GERBERG fans within striking distance of The New York Historical Society must check out their show, *Mort Gerberg Cartoons: A New Yorker's Perspective*, open until May 5. Mort also has a new book out from Fantagraphics: *On the Scene*, which skims the cream from his 50-year career.

Readers who appreciated **JOE CIARDIELLO**'s Western portraits last issue (I was partial to the one of Claudia Cardinale, for reasons too obvious to explain) can meet the man himself for a reading and Q&A at WORD in Jersey City, at 7:30 p.m. on April 18th. I'd be there, if I didn't have to squire my nieces and nephew around the sweltering asphalt hell of Disneyland.

I'm running out of space, so I'll just note a few last books of special interest. I still remember that afternoon in Wrigleyville when **KEN KRIMSTEIN** showed me pages-in-progress for *The Three Escapes of Hannah Arendt*. If things continue as they're going, Ken, those pages may end up in a museum. And in case you missed it, two Bystanders have recently published memoirs: **NELL SCOVELL**'s *Just the Funny Parts*, and **MIKE REISS**'s *Springfield Confidential*. If you're a Dante looking to explore modern television comedy, you could not find a better pair of Vergils. ◼

Cartoonist/director **NICHOLAS SPOONER** *(right) and friend model the t-shirt tie-in to our "Operation Waterfall" video, which Nick directed from a script by* **STEVE YOUNG**. *Go check it out on YouTube!*

DO YOU KNOW GINGER?

WE DO.

Created as the perfect conclusion to a great meal, Barrow's Intense is a cold pressed ginger liqueur, handcrafted in Brooklyn using more than 200lbs of fresh ginger per batch. Serve it over ice or add it to your favorite cocktail.

44 proof/22% ALC/VOL
Gluten Free, Vegan, Kosher Ⓚ

★ ★ ★ ★
4 Stars/Highly Recommended & Superb
F. Paul Pacult / Spirit Journal Sept 2014

A+
Good Spirits News

94
TASTING PANEL

"Best in Class"

BY SARA LAUTMAN

DOING JAZZ

"I'm always drawing the same five pointy animals."

"This is all just some big caption contest to you, isn't it?"

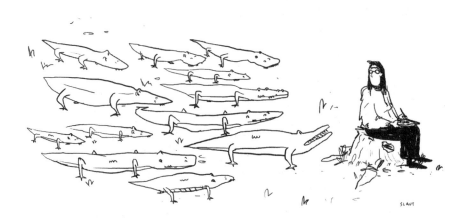

"Hey, you know those collective nouns are just a bunch of made up crap, right?"

"Look, just let me do it!"

"I'm called the Skin Horse because I'm made out of discrded human foreskin, okay? Got any more burning questions?"

SARA LAUTMAN
(Instagram: @slautow) is an artist in Baltimore. She contributes regularly to **The New Yorker** *and her most recent collection,* **I Love You,** *is available from Retrofit.*

CHRISTINA **HENDRICKS** ALYSIA **REINER** DAVID ALAN **BASCHE** WITH GBENGA **AKINNAGBE** AND ANNA **CAMP**

EGG

TRIBECA FILM FESTIVAL 2018 OFFICIAL SELECTION

"EXPLODES CLICHES ABOUT MOTHERHOOD, MARRIAGE AND CAREER."
— *The Hollywood Reporter*

2 WONDER FULL TO BE LTD & MO STUDIOS PRESENT CHRISTINA HENDRICKS ALYSIA REINER DAVID ALAN BASCHE WITH GBENGA AKINNAGBE AND ANNA CAMP A FILM BY MARIANNA PALKA "EGG" PRODUCED BY MICHELE GANELESS, PGA ALYSIA REINER, PGA DAVID ALAN BASCHE, PGA MUSIC BY WAZ-JACKSON EDITED BY SOPHIE CORRA DIRECTOR OF PHOTOGRAPHY ZELMIRA GAINZA PRODUCTION DESIGNER SALLY LEVI COSTUME DESIGNER JENN ROGIEN SCREENPLAY BY RISA MICKENBERG DIRECTED BY MARIANNA PALKA

Gallimaufry

When I was young, I wanted to change the world.
Then, I wanted to make a lot of money.
Now, I'd just like to stay out of jail.

THE METAMORPHOSIS (IN BRIEF).

A traveling salesman named Gregor
Awoke as a gruesome six-legger
He was finally finished
By a young violinist:
"Bug-Boy won't make *me* a beggar!"
—*Lance Hansen*

B.H. (BEFORE HAMILTON).

We Wolcott You *(2002)*—Lin-Manuel Miranda's senior project was an "extremely metal, pyrotechnic-heavy potboiler" (Wesleyan *Argus*) about Treasury Secretary Oliver Wolcott Jr. *WWY* closed after the male lead caught on fire during the cataclysmic eight-minute shredfest dramatizing Wolcott's 1788 appointment as comptroller to the State of Connecticut. *(One performance.)*

Don't Worry, Be Humphrey *(2004)*—A reggae interpretation of George M. Humphrey's tenure as 55th Treasury secretary. Miranda insisted the entire show be performed in authentic patois, leading to lines like, "*Wah-Gwan* President Eisenhower! The capital gains tax is *chaka-chaka*!" Out-of-town audiences were perplexed. *(Three performances.)*

Sweeney Cobb *(2009)*—A Grand Guignol portrait of 22nd Treasury Secretary Howell Cobb. Backers were horrified by a dance sequence where Cobb uses the blood of his victims to write out the equation for compound interest. *(Unproduced.)*

Houston, We Have s Secretary *(2011)*—Half meditation on Man's place in the Universe, half space odyssey about 48th Treasury Secretary David F. Houston. Miranda demanded that the entire production be performed on wires to create the illusion of zero gravity. Frequent accidents aside, some critics were enchanted, but most found this a peculiar choice to dramatize the Farm Loan Act of 1916. *(Five performances.)*

—*Adam Chase*

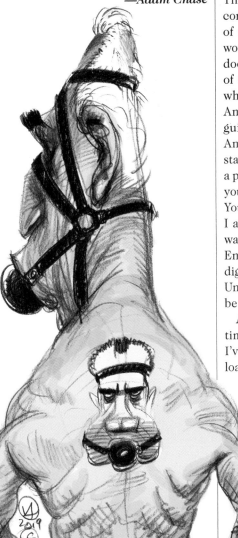

VICTOR JUHASZ

SO...WE MEET AGAIN!

I've been waiting a long time for this. And I think you'll find that *this* time, I am ready for you! Oh yes, this time, I shall exact my revenge!

This will not be like the last time! This time, I made sure that I had your correct address. We'll have no repeat of that unfortunate mistake, when I wound up pounding on your neighbor's door! I'm sure you recall the events of that day! How I didn't believe her when she said you didn't live there! And how I—certain it was you in disguise—tried to remove her "mask." And how, in the subsequent misunderstanding, she tased me. And then, when a police officer came, I thought *he* was you in disguise. And then *he* tased me. You weren't at the police station, but I assure you, once I was there, there was additional tasing. So much tasing. Enough tasing to last a lifetime! But I digress...there will be no tasing today! Unless it is me tasing you! But, just to be clear, I will not be tasing you.

And unlike the time before that, this time, my gun is loaded! Furthermore, I've made sure that this time, it is loaded with bullets! Not candy corns. You know how they say "never send a boy to do a man's job"? It turns out that loading a gun is a "man's job"—as my 7-year-old son and I both found out the hard way. I was upset about the lost bullets; he was upset about his lost candy corns. It was a tense car ride home, and I'm in no hurry to repeat it.

You'll also notice I've gotten rid of my nervous stutter! You'll

What I love about CANADA
• by Penny Barr © 2019 •

Canada, for so many reasons, is a veritable paradise on Earth. Being Canadian, we have tended to keep this to ourselves—until now!

We're building a wall too—out of empties * (Molson and Labatts mostly.) There's a caravan coming from the south for B.C. Bud and free health care.

Canadians are so polite; the strippers give you change.

Milk comes in plastic BAGS! Fiercely eco-friendly, they can also be used as delightfully cooling neck supports on long flights.
* Thank you, D. Edwards of T.O. ♥

My fellow Canadians: What do YOU love about Canada? Send your ideas to: pen.american bystander@gmail.com

recall how the fourth time we met, in my excitement, it took me a full three minutes to utter, "We m-m-mm-meet a-g-g-g-g-g-g-g-gain." Maybe you don't remember, since you shrugged your shoulders and walked away after 90 seconds, leaving me to finish my staccato threat towards the empty, mocking air! You no longer have that luxury, you rogue! Listen: "WE MEET AGAIN!" See how easily I've said it?

Thank you, Dr. Jantz! Your speech therapy has sealed this scoundrel's fate! *Mwah-haha-ha-ha-ha-ha-ha!* Yes, I still stutter when I laugh maniacally, but that's an issue we'll address in future sessions!

Unlike the sixth time we met, I will not be using an army of falcons to attack you. I now know that falcons have to be trained to attack—you can't just buy a bunch and assume that you and the birds are "all on the same page." I also learned that if your (not inexpensive) falcons fly off, never to be seen again, it's impossible to return them to the pet store. Even if you have the receipt. Not even for store credit.

Yes, I've learned from *all* my past mistakes and shall not be repeating any of them!

On the fifth time we met, I made the novice error of letting you beat me to within an inch of my life! History has been an excellent teacher, and I will not be falling into *that* trap again! Hence the inflatable sumo suit I'm wearing as I appear before you today!

I am also avoiding the dramatic gestures I've relied too heavily upon in the past.

You'll notice that, unlike last time, I'm not wearing a billowing cloak and twirling it in an ominous fashion! We both know how that turned out. I assure you, when I practiced my cloak-twirling in the mirror, it appeared quite threatening and sinister.

But you and I both know how life has a funny way of getting you entangled in your own cloak, making you trip, topple over and roll down a hill into a partially filled drainage ditch. By the way, I don't think I ever thanked you for helping to pull me out. *And I never will!*

Things will be quite different this time! I've planned for every eventuality and now I have you exactly where

I want you! Actually, could you move just a hair to your left?

Like, two feet? Right onto that giant X? The one in the shadow of that swaying baby grand piano? No?!? Bah! You win this round! But mark my words —we will meet again!

—*Dave Croatto*

TWO-SECOND MYSTERIES.

The curtains are fudgy, while across the room a toddler romps, brown-fingered.

*A **woman is found dead** in a puddle of water in her apartment, which is next door to an ice-knife store.

*A **successful businessman** disappears from his office one day, leaving behind only a printout of an e-ticket.

*A **man rushes his son** to the hospital, only to have the doctor there say,"I can't operate on my own son." Then she says, "Aw screw it, yes I can."

Phillip and Phillippa are mysteriously both found dead, in a room with no open doors or windows and also no oxygen.

Two strangers at a party come to realize they were on the same airplane fifteen years ago that crashed on a deserted island …because they are both fictional characters from the show "Lost."

—*Rob Kutner*

THE UNBEARABLE LIGHTNESS OF BEING (IN BRIEF).

A handsome young surgeon from
  Prague
Adrift in a philanderous fog
Between a girl in a bowler
And his wife (a bipolar)
Who spends most of her time
  with a dog.

—*Lance Hansen*

ELECTION ASSISTANCE.

A dimly lit empty room in a secret location. Two middle-aged, suburban parents, BOB and LISA, sit at a table across from DIMITRI, a Russian intelligence officer, a stolid, florid Slav

ALL DIALOGUE GUARANTEED VERBATIM

with a thick accent. Dimitri reads through a file, carefully, then looks up at them.

DIMITRI
Alright, Mr. and Mrs. — ?

LISA
Uh, Smith? We're not good at this.

DIMITRI
Let me see if I understand this correctly: You would like my organization to help your son Robby win the Piedmont High School election.

BOB
We want our boy to be junior class president.

LISA
We don't care what it takes.

DIMITRI
You don't think he could win on his own?

BOB
Robby? No way.

LISA
Not a chance in hell.

DIMITRI
Surely he has friends?

LISA
Our son is truly, truly disliked. That's why we stopped at one.

DIMITRI
And his academics?

BOB
Awful. His grades look like typos.

LISA
Skips most of his classes. Bottom quartile SATs.

BOB
Are you familiar with the American phrase "total fucking burnout"?

LISA
Bob, that's not fair. Even the burnouts don't like him. He *aspires* to be a burnout.

BOB
Oh, and he's a bully. And a stalker!

DIMITRI
Maybe he should come to work for us! I kid.

LISA
(laughs)
We thought about that.

BOB
Dmitri, you have to help us. If he doesn't do something, something *big*, he's never going to leave home.

LISA
Junior Class Prez — that would look *good* on the Common App.

BOB
We realize this is just a fishing trip, but…

Bob pulls out a briefcase and opens the lid. It's full of money. Dimitri grins.

DIMITRI
That is a lot of bait! *(beat)* All right, American soccer parents, there are many things we could do for your little "burn-up." Set up fake news sites showing various heroic exploits. Falsify testimonials from his classmates. How much they love him. How he is a worthy, brilliant leader of men.

UBER DRIVER WISDOM

by Ivan Ehlers

Deborah, 61 *(San Diego, CA)*: "I only drive Uber because my husband doesn't listen to me anymore. You have to listen to me. No matter how crazy I sound! Hey. You can't open the door while I'm driving."

Bobby, 41 *(Vancouver, WA)*: "They have two separate bathrooms at bars, but there should really be three. And they should be labeled: One for '#1.' Two for '#2.' Three for 'Drugs and/or Sex' or whatever people do in there that takes forever. Then you know how long you have to wait."

Garret, 56 *(Aurora, IL)*: "I'm not an attorney anymore, and this is not legal advice. But, I had to tell her: 'You can't sue a guy for thinking about you.' At least not yet!"

"*What?*"

LISA
And women.

DIMITRI
Yes, we would also make your Robby into a "cool" guy. A guy that "chicks dig"!

BOB
I don't think kids say "dig" —

DIMITRI
Don't worry, our linguists will take care of everything. The messaging will be perfect — then, we start the voter intimidation.

Lisa frowns.

DIMITRI
Don't worry, Soccer Mother. None of this would be traceable back to you.

BOB
Now that's customer service.

LISA
Could you do that thing where the pope endorses him? That would be so super!

DIMITRI
That was a good one, wasn't it?

BOB
So, when can we start?!

DIMITRI
Yes. Well, sadly, I cannot take this job.

Bob and Lisa look at Dimitri, shocked. Dimitri pulls out a headshot of a young, punky BOY with bad acne and braces.
Lisa gasps.

BOB
Doug Cole.

DIMITRI
His parents have already contracted with us.

LISA
Listen, whatever they paid you —

DIMITRI
Unfortunately, impossible. The operation's too far along. *(beat)* But if Robby would consider *vice* president…

Bob and Lisa look at each other, relieved, as we go to
BLACKOUT
—*Alex Bernstein*

CHANNELING YOUR FEMININE RAGE.

Start by creating a lifestyle blog. You'll be able to seamlessly integrate your anger into a post sharing a seasonal cookie recipe, which everyone will quickly scroll through to figure out if they can substitute walnuts for pecans. They cannot, but they will anyway.

Cross-stitch your rage into a pillow. Have the pillow say something inspirational and relatively unassertive.

Think, "Nevertheless, She Persisted" or "She Believed She Could, So She Did" or "I Made This Because I Am Fine And Not Angry At All!!!!" Don't forget to post process pictures on your lifestyle blog, which is now your primary source of income.

A wonderful thing about being furious, in a ladylike way, is your body will eventually condense into a healing crystal. If you're lucky, you might turn into one that's pink and sparkly! Speaking of crystals, self-care is crucial if you're looking to balance your feminine rage. Do face masks. Utilize moisturizing creams. Buy oils, clays, silly puttys to fill in all your premature fury wrinkles. Your skin will look so good that maybe you'll forget all about whatever was making you angry in the first place, but probably not.

If your blood is boiling from a news-induced fury, use your head as a steamer and make some dumplings. Given the state of our environment, finding ways to recycle energy is essential. Plus, dumplings taste good! You can find my favorite dumpling recipe on my blog, *Now We're Cooking With Fire I Started Just By Staring At The Morning Newspaper*.

Despite what culture and catcallers tell you, you don't have to smile if you don't feel like it. Unless—and this is important—you're taking bridesmaids pictures for Heather. Then you better smile, goddamnit. It's her day, and she will crop you out of photos and not feel bad at all. Maybe just act like Heather did on her wedding day? She had no problem asking for exactly what she wanted. Plus, she ended up getting her way and people only called her "bridezilla" for, like, six months.

Say how you're feeling. Don't be afraid to express that anger so long as you do it in a secluded forest where no one is around to hear you and ask why you're overreacting. If a woman is angry and no one is around to hear it, does she make a sound? No one knows or will ever find out and that's a good thing!

When you're feeling particularly enraged and can't make it to the woods, scream into a throw pillow. This will feel extra satisfying if it's the one you cross-stitched. If you don't have a handmade throw pillow, this will also work with couch cushions, bath towels, Target brand infinity scarves, a handful of beauty blenders, some socks bundled together, or a big, fluffy dog.

Ultimately, one of the best ways to channel your feminine rage is to keep tangible record of how you're feeling. Write it down, preferably in pretty, loopy handwriting. Seal it in an envelope, put the envelope in an airtight box, and bury the box in the ground. Generations from now, researchers will discover the box with your letter tucked inside. Anthropologists will study the message, now an artifact of feminine rage. They'll will have it preserved, protected and hung it in a history museum, adorned with the label, "Written by some angry old bitch."

Oh, that reminds me! Make sure to check out my blog post on calligraphy as an act of resistance. Bonus points if you use your own rage sweat as ink!

—*Mia Mercado*

THE REASON WE HIRED HIM.

We had all decided that J. Daimler was the perfect choice to play Mungus. In fact, his face might even have been the inspiration for Mungus in the first place. It has since become difficult to ascertain, in light of everything that has transpired, if there were other factors in play.

The trouble started the first day J. Daimler was on set. He destroyed the craft services table, made a lewd gesture at one of the boom operators, then locked himself in his trailer in the aftermath of a brutally contentious lunch. Things escalated quickly, feelings were hurt, resignations were proffered, agents were contacted, producers called in from the coasts.

Still, we were in the presence of genius.

On the morning of the second day, J. Daimler showed up with a heavy grocery bag that he carried like a bowling ball. I knew no good could come from whatever he had in the bag. Halfway through his first scene, he walked calmly over to me and slammed a pie tin full of lead weights right in my face.

I awoke the next day in a hospital bed. One of the producers, M. Forienz,

Henrik, 50 *(Little Armenia, CA)*: "I don't speak any English. My brother got me this job." *[Google Translated from Armenian]*

Ariel, 34 *(Nashville, TN)*: "Nobody normal would own a snake. My uncle owned a snake. And he definitely was not normal."

Marvin, 33 *(Hollywood, FL)*: ""We didn't have sex, but—we almost got to sex! I mean, everything but sex. So mostly, basically sex. Which is practically sex. So close to sex. And that wasn't even the best ride I ever gave!"

Toofan, 59 *(Queens, NY)*: "I only sleepwalk to stay in shape."

Deborah, 61 *(San Pedro, CA)*: "I want to squat when I'm using a public toilet, but I lack the core strength. I start and if I'm not done in under three or four seconds, I am sitting down. PLOP! I don't care how dirty the seat is. I am simply not strong enough. Stop trying to open the door while I'm driving. It's child-proofed."

Gloria, 23 *(Whittier, CA)*: "I know I look sleepy, but don't worry. It's just my fake eyelashes that are heavy (just kidding). But, no really, it's just my fake eyelashes (just kidding). I like wearing them because it makes my eyes look half-open and guys think I'm giving them sexy bedroom eyes and they, like, tip way more for my rides (just kidding). But, no really: They really do. For serious."

Jeremy, 36 *(Flint, MI)*: "Einstein was an idiot and he knows it. Everything that he supposedly predicted is wrong and I don't care if 'modern equipment' supposedly proves anything. One day,

"What sick person would chop your mom into pieces and make you wear her?"

was at my side, advising me to seek legal counsel. He said that with a little luck, my eyesight would be restored. Meanwhile, the part of Mungus would be recast.

I bolted up in my bed. "But why?"

"The unconscionable behavior of J. Daimler, of course! He is a monster, he must not be allowed—"

"But Forienz!" I protested. "That's the reason we hired him!"

—*Jeffrey Kulik*

BOWLING WITH THE FÜHRER.

"Bowling. But the Führer is the master of that, too."

—From *The Diary of Joseph Goebbels*, ed. Elke Fröhlich.

September 1, 1936
Dear Diary,
Do you remember how smart Hitler is? (Of course you do.)

Today I was at an important meeting with all sorts of important Nazis (and Göring). We were having a super-tense argument about army stuff, when all of the sudden Hitler says: "Stop. Just stop, roll up the maps of the Rhineland. Look at us, we're all super-stressed. We have to relax or we will *burn out*" and I know that he was thinking of me in particular because he knows just how hard I've been working lately. I mean,

everybody knows that.

"Let's play a game," the Führer says. The room is skeptical, but he charms them with threats and cajoling. And then he turns to me. "Come on, Goebbels, think of something, you're fun." And then everybody laughs, because they know: I am the most fun.

So I think inside my head, I say to myself, "Joseph, we are talking about Hitler here. *The* Hitler. And he's right. We've been basically working nonstop since Kristallnacht. Even Göring has been pulling his weight, which is really saying something. (I'm saying he is fat and lazy.)

What is the perfect game for our moment? A game that is fun, relaxing, and not at all Jewish?

"Bowling," I say.

But no one reacts. So "BOWLING!" I shout.

What a bold idea!, Hitler thought (but judged unwise to say).

Göring though—poor, Göring!—is a flabby man with weak vision. "Bowling," he says. "Do you have a ball and pins stuffed under that oversized jacket, or are you just dumb?"

(Diary, I want you to know the jacket is big. But as I have been performing daily calesthenics my chest and arms will soon grow *enormous*. Meanwhile poor Göring will one day suffocate in all those chins. Seven and counting.)

Now I am definitely not stupid. But while bowling was the perfect choice, there were crucial details that required attention: Pins, and balls. I thoroughly considered the options.

"Would someone slap Goebbels on the head?" said Hitler. "He's making his 'thinking' sound."

I saw (non-Jewish) stars, but that was exactly the slap I needed. I went to the map table and gathered all the empty ginger ale bottles. (Göring had two.) I then grabbed the globe off the desk. I left these at Hitler's feet as if to say, look, here is your world: *Take it!* Also here are some empty bottles: *Take these too!*

"This is why I keep Goebbels around," our Hitler said, beaming. My proudest moment!!

We play, and you wouldn't guess who won. Just kidding: Of course you can! (It was Hitler.) Hitler bowled so well that everyone else forfeited.

"See that's what I mean," said Hitler. "This was *fun*."

At that, I went deep into thought. The pins falling, one by one, like the nations of the world. And our mighty Wehrmacht, rolling like a massive ball. World domination? Bowling. But the Führer is the master of that, too. The thought gives me much pleasure, and I smile.

"God, that sound again," says Hitler. "Göring, would you?"

—*Michael Pershan*

NO EXIT (IN BRIEF).

Garcin, Inez and Estelle—
Three souls sharing one room in hell
Garcin half-jokes:
"Hell's other folks"
And the Valet never answers the bell!
—*Lance Hansen*

I AM A WRITER, PLEASE DON'T MAKE ME WRITE.

I am a professional writer.

What makes me a writer? Well, a lot of it is typewriters and sentences and knowing where words go, but I think most of it is that I hate writing more than anything in the world and please don't make me do it.

Some writers say that they actually enjoy writing, almost all of the time. But don't be fooled: These are not real writers! Real writers know that complaining about writing is to the writer what water is to the body: a full 75 percent of it.

Writing is a magical process. I start every morning with a blank page, and then a mere four hours later, through the miracle of the written word, I have organized all my socks by thread count.

To write is to engage in the most sacred of professions. As a writer, every day, I explain the unexplainable; I craft worlds with my fingertips; I sit in front of my laptop and scream "NO!" at a blank page for a full thirty minutes before taking a nap.

I am truly living the dream. Every day since I became a writer, I wake up each morning, take a deep breath of air, and realize—with grateful tears in my eyes—that I would rather walk across a room of a cyanide Legos than write a single goddamn word.

I love to write when I don't HAVE to do it! It's just that forcing myself to write is like pulling teeth, which is a simile, which is a magical trick of writing, which is literally the job of my dreams/thing I hate more than anything in the universe.

When I say things like this, people always ask me: If you chose to be a writer, should doing your job really feel like pulling teeth? I find this comes from a place of ignorance, so I answer that question with another question: Would you still be asking me that if I were a dentist?

Maybe it's not entirely accurate to say that I hate writing. It's more that every minute of my horrible, amazing, bitter, blessed life where I am forced (by no one) to pursue my highest calling feels like a Sophie's Choice between writing and not writing. To not write would kill me! To write would also kill me! So instead I choose the middle road, which is to watch *Sophie's Choice*, and after that, *The Devil Wears Prada*, and then after that, maybe the one about the dingos. And after that, I buy myself a new Moleskine because I have earned it.

Should I just stop writing if I hate it so much? What a silly question!

equipment will be really modern and you'll see. Everyone will see. Do you even know what a Planck length is? Probably not. You'd have your own car if you did."

Al, 50 *(Bed-Stuy, NY)*: "A pansexual is someone who can have sex with anyone for five minutes, but no one for ten. If you have the time, I have the energy."

Duane, 50 *(Kansas City, MO)*: "I ate jalapeños for lunch. That's why my face is red. That's why you're in 'Smell Hell.' That's why I feel pain from my belly to my head. My gums hurt. My teeth hurt. My throat hurts. My heart hurts. My fingernails hurt. The linings of my intestines hurt. Uh-oh. You'd better roll down your window again."

Dave, 48 *(Dayton, OH)*: "My hair is nothing to write home about, but it used to really kick ass. Used to be business in the front and party in the back. The party's still rocking in the back, but the boys in front went out of business a long time ago. That's how come I wear this beanie even when it's hot out."

Klaus, 64 (*Cape Town, South Africa*): "I hate nature. Nature is hell. I hate the beach. The only reason I go to the beach is to see the women in bikinis. That's it!"

Deborah, 61 (*San Pedro, CA*): ""I know, I know: The plane's taking off soon. Listen, if you do miss the flight, which I'm not saying you are, but if you do, you have to check the news later to see if the flight you would have been on crashed or got infected with some diseases. If it did, then guess what? I just saved your life! Which is worth at least a 5-star rating! Hey—how'd you get the door open?" **B**

Writing is the one singular joy in my life, and I don't see why it matters that most of the time I would rather gnaw off my own arm than do it.

Even when it's difficult, writing stretches me in important ways. For example, I think it is GOOD that I spent 40 full minutes agonizing over whether it flowed better to say "gnaw off my own arm" or "gnaw my own arm off" until I got a stress headache and had to lie down. In many ways, that exact scenario is what I always dreamed of as a little girl!

That reminds me that I have wanted to be a writer since I was in second grade, and now here I am! I'm really doing it! I like to imagine traveling back in time and saying to that little girl: Look! We did it! We became a writer! And then I like to picture the look of disappointment on her face as she learns that instead of the future career that she imagined, which was something of a mashup between writer and world's first bottlenose dolphin expert/professional Skip-It! Athlete, her actual future career is as an unshowered introvert who writes SEO-optimized blog content for procurement executives at midsized multifamily housing units.

Does the fact that I haven't actually written anything in years mean that I'm not a real writer? How dare you. If someone had never planned or built a building, but still spent all of their time obsessively thinking things

like, "I should really be architecting right now," or, "Come on, just plan 100 square feet of a building, that's it, and then you can take a break," would you accuse them of not being a real architect?! Actually, yes, probably, now that I'm thinking about it.

If I'm really honest, of course, it isn't all bad. There are some days when writing is pure bliss: when I'm really in a groove, when the words are just flying. On those days, there's nothing I love more. But then I have to log out of my wildly unpopular Peppa Pig/Paw Patrol fanfic blog and get back to work.

Ultimately, for all of writing's difficulties, I would still say this to any aspiring writer out there: Find a job you love and you'll never work a day in your life. Find a job you hate, like writing, and you'll also never work a day in your life, but for very different reasons.

—*Riane Konc*

THE LORD OF THE FLIES (IN BRIEF).

Young survivors split up into cliques
Got naked and sharpened their stiques
Soon these war-painted kids
Really let loose their ids
And eventually killed Piggy for kiques.

—*Lance Hansen* **B**

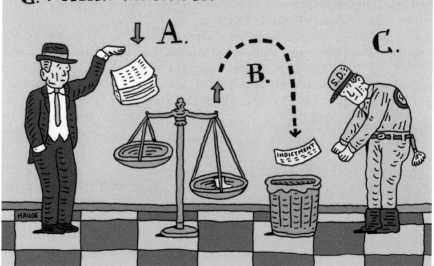

A. MUELLER DROPS FINAL REPORT ON SCALES OF JUSTICE.
B. JUSTICE DEPT. BURIES REPORT, CLEARS PRESIDENT.
C. MUELLER REASSIGNED.

RON HAUGE

A Fistful of Drawings
A Graphic Journal by Joe Ciardiello

*A paean to Hollywood, a love letter to the Western,
and a tribute to its Italian influences.*

In this gorgeous graphic memoir, Joe Ciardiello
gracefully weaves together his Italian family
history and the mythology of the American
West while paying homage to the classic movie
and TV Westerns of the '50s and '60s. Featuring
Ciardiello's signature sinuous ink line and vivid
watercolors, *A Fistful of Drawings* illuminates
the oversized characters that dominated the
cinematic American West—Clint Eastwood
John Ford, John Wayne, Claudia Cardinale,
Sophia Loren, and many more.

*"Joe Ciardiello has been one of America's
finest artists for the last generation. Here we
finally have his magnum opus: a project that
brilliantly blends mid-century culture, the
Italian-American experience, and his own
personal story into something rare in form,
unique in content, and startlingly deep in
every nuance. It is a work of genius."*

**—Steve Brodner
Illustrator/political satirist**

Claudia Cardinale

"...FANS OF PARANORMAL THRILLERS WILL BE SATISFIED"
—PUBLISHERS WEEKLY

Settle back and savor this one. Plenty of sizzle and emotional clout...a
barrage of breathless, cross-cutting suspense.
—STEVE BERRY,
New York Times bestselling author of *The Bishop's Pawn*

THE GHOST MANUSCRIPT

KRIS FRIESWICK

BY LUCAS GARDNER

ATTENTION RESIDENTS:

Yes, yes…but is it rent-controlled?

JONATHAN PLOTKIN

We will be doing maintenance on the building this week. We apologize in advance for any noise. Beginning tomorrow at 4:30 a.m., there will be some routine work done on the building's ventilation system. You might hear loud banging in your ceilings and/or walls.

We'll also be testing for mold in the main corridor in the early, early morning. If we find any, we will buzz your apartment to wake you up and let you know. We'll also buzz you if we don't find any.

Due to some water pressure issues, we need to de-clog the building's pipes. We'll need to take all the pipes out and bang them against each other until all the junk gets knocked out of there. We will be doing this in the hallway shortly before sunrise. We apologize once again for the noise but this is the funnest way to de-clog the pipes.

We'll also be doing some rewiring, and the building will need to be hooked up to a fairly loud generator at that time. This generator will be hooked up to a P.A. system for reasons to be decided later.

We'll also be testing out a new fire alarm system that sounds whenever there isn't a fire, and stops when there is one.

Due to overflow in the building's recycling bins, we will be smashing glass bottles out back before sunrise to make them fit in the bins better. This will also be noisy and unfortunately will coincide with us replacing all the windows in the building, which no one requested.

Due to a recent issue with bugs, there will be some light extermination work done in the morning as well. This will be conducted by my nephew Howlin' Larry, The Exterminator Who Screams When He Sees Bugs™.

Per a suggestion from an anonymous person, who we're not entirely sure if they live in the building or not, we will be installing new toilets that are extremely loud when you flush them. The installation process itself will be very loud as well.

We will be drilling into the sidewalk out front with jackhammers all morning. This is a necessary action that we must take in order to determine which of our many jackhammers we love the best.

As a courtesy, I've booked a guy to come wail on the bagpipes all morning to drown out the noise.

Once again, maintenance will be conducted Saturday morning around 4:30 a.m., so do not be alarmed by any noise. Also, rent is going up 8%.

Your superintendent,
Lucas   B

LUCAS GARDNER *(@Lucas_Gardner) is a staff writer for the TBS series* **Miracle Workers.** *He's the author of two comic novels,* **Quietly, From Afar…** *and* **Contemptible Blue,** *and lives in Queens.*

BY PETER SALOMONE

NO, YOU CANNOT HAVE YOUR ORGY AT THE MUSEUM

Thank you for your repeated inquiries regarding museum event space rental. The Aaron K. Danning Museum of Natural History is very proud of the wide variety of events we host; each year, many groups throughout Central Florida experience "an evening that will live in History."

I regret to inform you that we must decline your request to host your orgy at the museum.

First, sanitation. It's not as simple as "steam-cleaning a few dioramas." The Danning Museum is home to many valuable historic artifacts; these are often fragile and definitely not body-safe. For most, "a quick wipe-down with Pine-Sol" would probably do more harm than good. I would not even be commenting on this issue had you not, in your last email, gone into troubling detail about your expectation and desire that the orgy be particularly "messy" and crescendo with a "human Slip 'N Slide."

Second, access. "Slipping [us] a few extra bucks" would certainly not grant you the ability to interact with any of our artifacts, especially not in the manner you're hoping for. And while food is indeed permitted in the event space, it must be arranged through one of our licensed and approved catering partners. I cannot think of a single vendor who would be able to provide baked goods in the shapes you've described.

Third, safety. It is quite impossible to hang multiple "Fetish Fantasy Gyroscopic SeXXX Swings" in the Time & Tides Room. We do often hang nature models, but the cables we use are designed to support, for example, a hollow fiberglass model of a brown pelican. These would not support the weight of several adults "writhing together in floating spheres of sweat and stink." Have you even calculated the torque and other forces involved in your hoped-for "frenzy of rut"? I want you to know that I did my due diligence in bringing this particular request to our insurance representative, who promptly informed me that it would not be possible to accommodate, even if we followed your suggestion of a "super hardass waiver."

Our Board of Directors rejected outright your suggestion that the museum's support of such an event could open up "a whole new revenue stream." (I'm not 100 percent sure what you're implying with that underlining, but I suspect it's highly inappropriate.) Speaking frankly, we have enough trouble as it is contending with patrons indulging in, shall we say, horseplay. You'd be surprised by how many people's passions are inflamed by a 13-minute documentary about the moon landing.

Your proposal to film the orgy and "allow [us] to sell Blu-rays in the gift shop" is thoughtful. However, our all-time best-selling video remains Grand Canyon Adventure and I think it would pretty hard for your orgy video to compete with that, especially considering the second half is practically all cute animals. (Before you write back: I know what furries are, the whole Board does, and: no.)

You mention an untapped audience "using the museum on nights and weekends." However, we already have patrons who use the museum during those times, and they are not "boundary-bustin' orgasmi-nauts." They are elementary school classes participating in our museum sleepover program. A double-booking during that time would be catastrophic.

Finally, your invitation for me to participate in the orgy is flattering, if not a bit of a Hail Mary. Unbeknownst to all but a select few docents, my personal prowess (which encompasses every possible orientation) is so advanced that the coital skills of the other participants would likely pale in comparison. To be sure, my involvement would be thrilling at first... but ultimately it would cast an embarrassing pall over the whole event. I would leave unsatisfied, and the other participants would feel so inadequate that the majority of them would retreat to a life of celibacy. This is not mere boasting; I spend one evening per week responding to emails and handwritten letters I receive from dejected former partners. They write me seeking guidance, perspective, and often another chance "to reach Nirvana once more before [they] die." (That is a direct quote.) It always ends the same: me, staring up at the ceiling, suspended in melancholy; he/she/them, curled up beside me, weeping ecstatically.

I'm sorry that we are not able to accommodate your request. As a consolation, please accept the attached printable free passes to our new exhibit, "Tides of the Ocean." And think of me, alone, trapped in a gray sexual purgatory none can possibly imagine.   B

PETER SALOMONE *(@pscottsalo) created The Walk of Life Project web series and was a creative consultant on Mike Birbiglia's* **The New One** *on Broadway. He is also an amateur cryptozoologist.*

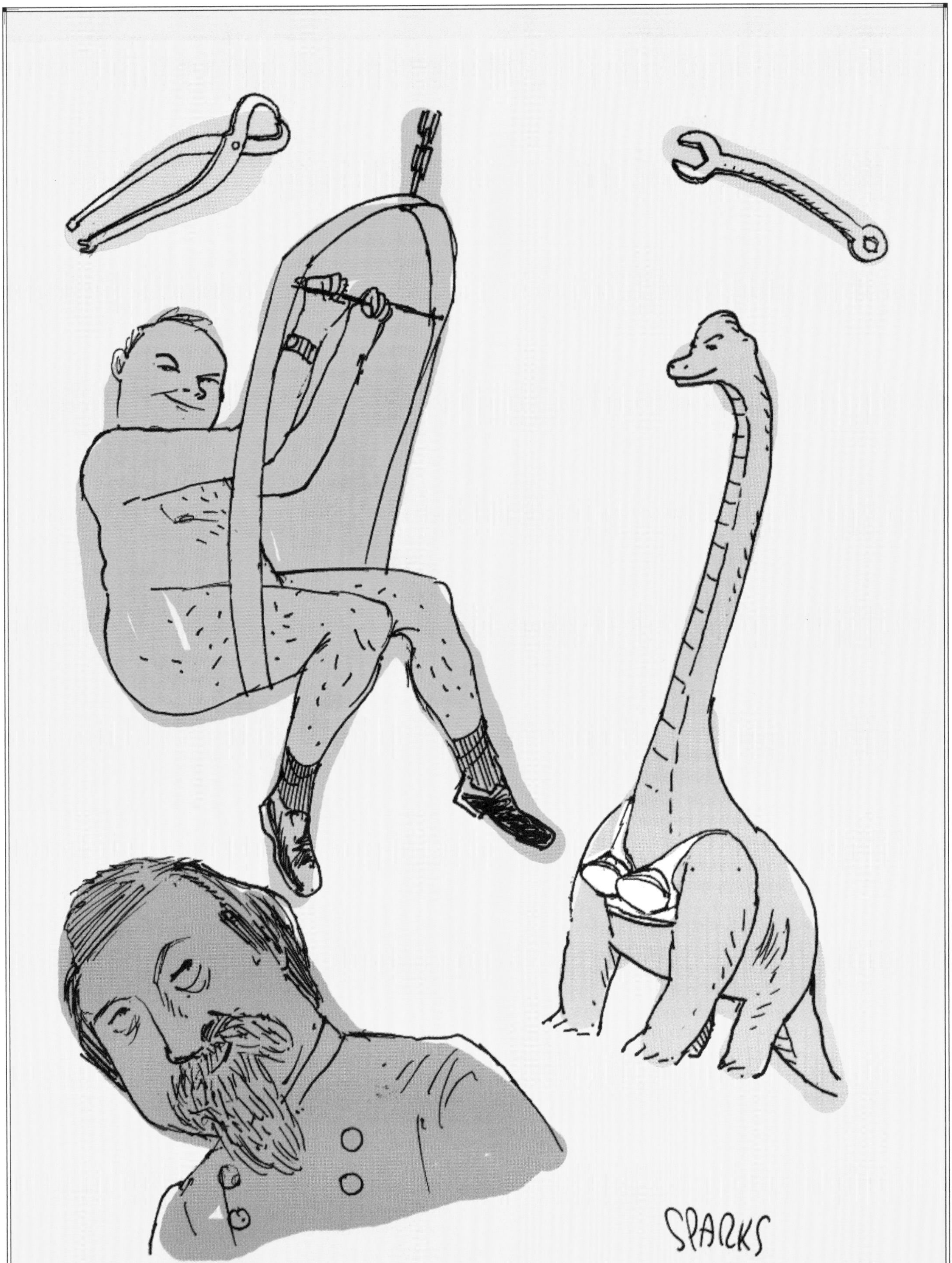
SPARKS

BY IKENNA AZUIKE

THE GREATEST EVER BRITAIN IN THE HISTORY OF BRITAINS!

Every day that passes moves the U.K. one step closer to a no-deal Brexit. By the time you read this, it may well be goodbye Europe and hello to—oh, nothing much… Just The Greatest Ever Britain In The History of Britains!

Sure, for a while, food will be more expensive, there'll be less of it on supermarket shelves and fewer medicines will be available, but Britons will have each other. Well, parts of each other—we may end up having to eat the weaker among us. But why focus on the negatives when there is so much to be happy about? We have a government that *truly cares*. When Health Secretary Matt Hancock said that the government would prioritize medicines over food in the case of a no-deal Brexit, that could mean only one thing: We'll all be fit and healthy enough to take part in the food riots! *Huzzah!* And since we never, not really, came to terms with losing our Empire in the first place, this is the perfect opportunity to grab it all up again.

Backwards is the new forwards! *Huzzah and Hurrah!*

Backward thinking has gotten a bad rap. Just look at the mavericks who opposed the Enlightenment and wanted to moonwalk all the way back to medieval times. If they'd been given a chance, would the world be in the mess it's in today? Of course not. Life expectancy would peak at 35, and that's a massive saving on health care costs for the elderly. Streets covered in shit and piss would be normal, so our immune systems would be nice and strong (maybe even strong enough to beat the inevitable return of bubonic plague). And with far fewer people traveling from country to country, there'd be no immigrants—meaning we'd be able to get our hands dirty again instead of Netflixing from the couch.

For anyone still possessing even a micron of doubt whether we should restore the British Empire, consider these indisputable facts:

• *Sports.* Back in the day, our Empire contained 23 percent of the world's total population. With that many "Brits" to choose from, we may finally win another World Cup.

• *Culture.* Once again, it'll be okay to *borrow* priceless artworks and precious stones from our colonies, and park them in our museums.

• *Leisure-Time Activities.* Women won't be able to vote or drive a car—*sorry*—but British men will finally be *men* again. We won't have to sit in cafes in front of laptops, sipping cappuccinos, silently weeping. Now we can *fight*. Other men. Perhaps even with swords. While dressed in coats of armour adorned with phallic symbols to remind everyone (at all times) of our boundless British masculinity.

• *More Leisure-Time Activities.* Britons were already the most attractive people on earth, but now that we'll have the Island to ourselves, marrying off our cousins, nephews and nieces to one another will virtually guarantee a pure and beautiful gene pool. Truly, we will be a Tinder paradise, the envy of the dating world.

• *Fashion.* Every male Briton will be issued a pith helmet, khakis, long brown socks and boots. Maybe even gaiters will come back. And it'll be compulsory for moustaches to be as bushy as a badger's balls.

• *Language.* We'll bring back glorious idioms that should never have gone out of fashion like "Fart Catcher," meaning a valet or footman, or "Driggle-Draggle"—a delightful term for a messy woman.

• *Slavery.* And because even the Greatest Britain can't be Great for everyone, we might even bring back slavery. I know, I know, but hear me out on this one. For one thing, it'll be a huge relief to government—no more pressure to try and improve the economy. Lest we forget: The Great British Empire was not exactly a cheery period for most folk in it. Did we care then? No. Should we care now? Also, no. Basic human rights are *bloody expensive*.

So, while Europe moves forward with its fancy motorways packed with electric, driverless cars, trying to save the planet and enjoying strange hobbies like peace and solidarity, we in Britain will revert to the good old days. We will travel by packhorse, fight with swords and eat Jaffa cakes for tea.

I hope all Britons will therefore join me in raising their (for now) metaphorical swords and issuing a simultaneous, pre-emptive ululation of war in the vague direction of all our ex-colonies. Ladies and gents, we are coming for you. In 2019, we will forge The Greatest Ever Britain In The History of Britains!

Hurrah! Huzzah! Look out! B

IKENNA AZUIKE *(@ikennaazuike) is a British-Nigerian-Dutch documentary presenter, producer and writer for the BBC and elsewhere. His BBC show* **What's Up Africa** *is available online.*

FESTIVAL OF BREXIT BRITAIN

GUIDE PRICE £120 MILLION*

RICHARD · LITTLER · AFTER · ABRAM · GAMES

*SUBJECT TO INFLATING JINGOISM

With apologies to Abram Games's iconic poster for the 1951 Festival of Britain, here's **RICHARD LITTLER**'s *design for a Festival of Brexit Britain.*

BY KHADJIAH JOHNSON

SHOULD I TELL MY WHITE CO-WORKER THIS BLACK JOKE?

Hello fellow black human! We've all been there: A spontaneous joke about the black experience is really funny, and you must share it with everyone. It could be about seasoning, slavery, police brutality, or on-beat dancing. But while checking off all the black friends on your contact list, you come across a non-melenated acquaintance, and the eternal question rears its Nordic head: *Should I share this joke with Fiona from Finance?*

STEP ONE: HOW WHITE ARE THEY?

The first question you must ask is how white are they? Are they a Tofu Tommy, the mysterious white, whose responses are so uncomfortable you keep HR on speed-dial and have a secret closet just in case? Or are they more a Turnip Tanya, the barely-woke white? Someone who skips the N-word during rap songs, but can't stay on-beat while doing so?

There's no getting around it: You must analyze the type of white. Not analyzing thoroughly will create awkward situations, and you'll end up in one of two conversations: A) Explaining that "reverse racism" does not exist, or B) trying to bridge an awkward silence by bringing up a white favorite, John Mulaney.

Clues are everywhere. How often, for example, does said white person use Urban Dictionary? If it's more than five times a week, chances are they shouldn't be using it at all. If they hear "Gang Gang Gang" and their first reaction is to duck, you probably shouldn't send them the joke. If you're having a discussion about "edges" and they pull out a geometry textbook—not only do they not deserve edges, they might even try and touch your hair. And you don't need that kind of energy, especially when you worked so hard on your twist out last night.

STEP TWO: HOW BLACK IS THIS JOKE?

Having analyzed the white in question, the next question becomes the blackness of the joke. Determine as best you can the severity, the texture, the relative wokeness. A three-star woke joke might be a level four on their cringe scale. One moment your hearty holler is sailing across the office, and the next second Kristen, Kurt and Kathy are apologizing for the Triangular Trade.

You might want to start with easy stuff, a simple giggle unlikely to scare away your cauliflower companion—like something about the blandness of white food. A meme, perhaps, showing a plain roast chicken captioned: "Classic White Dinner." It's easy to understand, proven throughout history… and might actually do some good in the world. Mayonnaise Mandy might be inspired to ditch the raisins and go to the seasoning rack to pick up some parsley.

Having put over such lighthearted stuff, you could move on to more complex cackles, e.g.:
- Seeing a shirt that's one hundred percent cotton and saying, "I'm not picking this one."
- Pulling sheets out of the dryer, and asking a white friend to try them on to see if they're clean enough.
- Your white friend proposing a cruise, and you shooting back: "That's what they said the last time."

To fellow colored folk, each of these might be a knee-slapper. But to our pasty pals, they might be met with blank stares—or worse. One must tread softly; "Fionas from Finance" always be snitchin' to the supervisor. An offhand joke might create a revolution in the office, something like a Gluten-Free Taco Tuesdays or No Appropriation Fridays.

If your Yogurt Yes-Man does not pass these tests, don't worry too much; just send the joke to your other black friends, and feel the joy from their reactions. White folk don't need to feel black joy all the time. In those rare cases where you might not have any black co-workers, keep the joke to yourself. In general, refrain from being the token black on the company's diversity pamphlets—unless they're giving you that Reparations Bonus.

Or you could be saucy and send it to them anyway. Why? Because white people don't have to always laugh at the joke; at times you just need to drag them. They're still prospering from the system their ancestors put in place over centuries, so there's nothing wrong with making the Jacuzzi a bit too hot.　　　　　**B**

KHADJIAH JOHNSON *(@iamkdjiah) is a writer and performer from Brooklyn. Her work has touched Madison Square Garden, Lincoln Center, and your mother's sweet heart.*

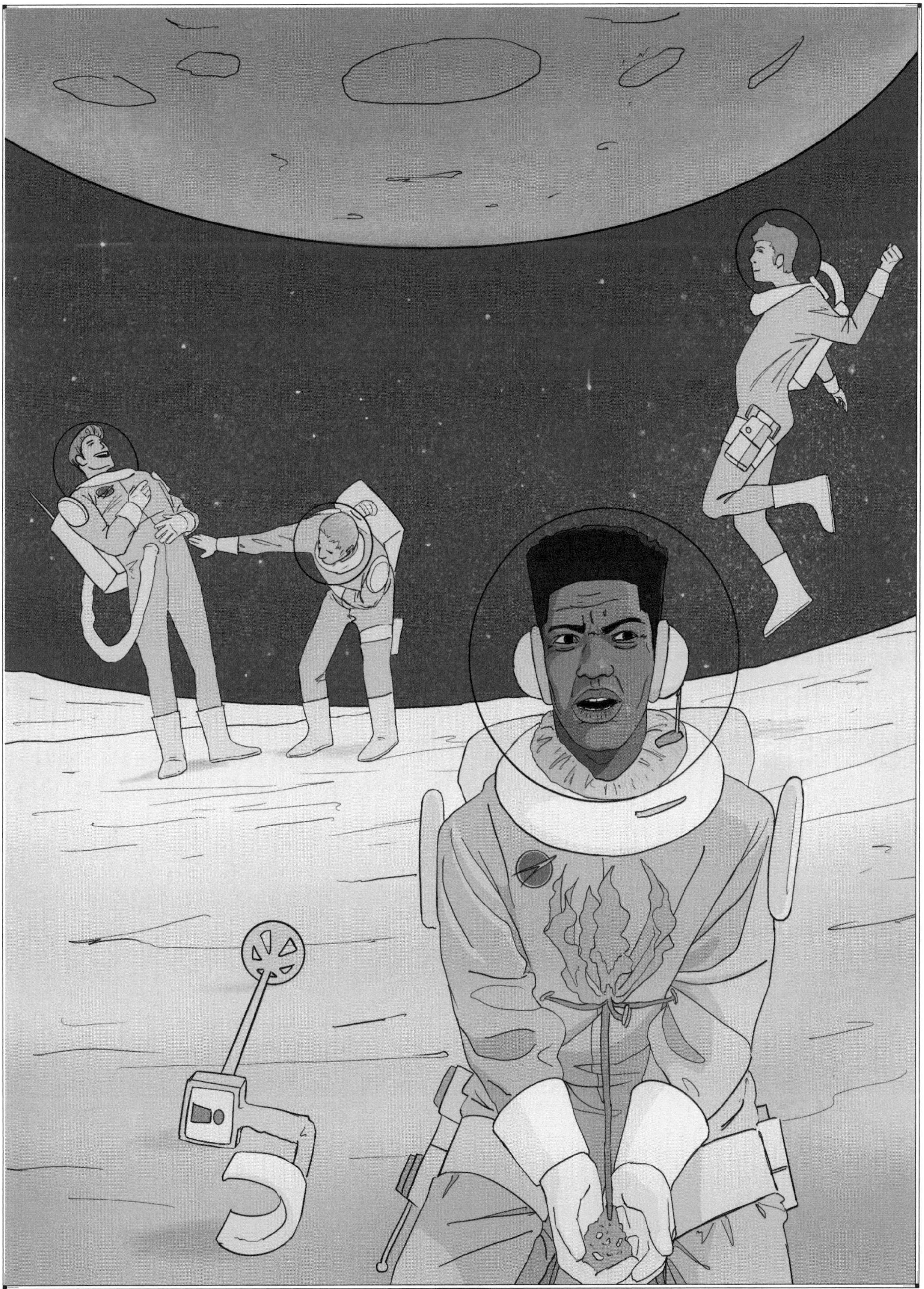

BY RIANE KONC

WHO ARE THE DEMOCRATIC SOCIALISTS OF AMERICA?

Bolstered by the popularity of politicians like Senator Bernie Sanders and Congresswoman Alexandria Ocasio-Cortez, the Democratic Socialists of America are getting more and more media attention. But just who are the DSA, and what do they believe? Here's a beginner's guide.

Democratic socialists believe that the ethical way to fund massive social programs is by taxing the rich. But that does not mean that they consider themselves modern-day Robin Hoods. In fact, the DSA's only official stance on the mythical figure of Robin Hood is that the cartoon fox who once played him is empirically attractive and it's not weird to have a crush on him.

The DSA often cites the success of social welfare programs in western European and Scandinavian countries as proof of democratic socialism's potential. Of course, Scandinavia has given us many other wonderful things, including winter Olympic sports that take too long and the "joyless female detective in sensible shoes solving grisly snow-murders" genre of television.

When the DSA talks about programs like universal preschool, they don't just mean for preschool-aged children. The DSA believes that every U.S. citizen needs to sit through a year of preschool, jammed into a child-sized chair like Billy Madison, until they learn how to share.

DSA members often use a rose emoji in their Twitter name. This is to signify that their children are doing a Valentine's Day fund-raiser for their school, which is a new thing, but like the PTA president said, it's either roses or magazine subscriptions again, and everyone was like, "Ugh, let's just do roses," so the point is, if anyone around the office wants to pitch in and buy a stem or two, that would be really helpful because if my daughter sells a certain amount she gets to spin this big prize wheel at an assembly or something.

Wow, no, the DSA actually hasn't heard of Venezuela, but trust that you bring this up in good faith, so please do go on.

One of the major benefits of belonging to the DSA is that you can tell your friends that you don't want to play Monopoly with them because, as a celebration of capitalism, it violates your principles, instead of telling them the truth, which is that Monopoly sucks and is boring, and also that this whole Thursday night game night thing feels more like a chore than anything at this point, and seems like it exists solely as a sad gesture to a once-vibrant friend group that really doesn't have much in common anymore, and you know what? Everyone knows it but is too afraid to just come out and say it.

A simplified way of thinking about the beliefs of the DSA is that they believe that everyone should get an equal slice of the pie, unless the pie in question is key lime, which the DSA has long held makes their mouths feel pinchy.

Ultimately, the DSA believes that a person's access to healthcare or education or housing should not be contingent on a person's being wealthy. The DSA believes that the only thing that should be contingent on wealth is the ability to use "summer" as a verb.

And finally, despite the popularity of the Rousseau quote, democratic socialists do not actually want to "eat the rich." But if they ordered some for the table, would anyone want to split? B

RIANE KONC *(@theillustrious) writes for* **The New Yorker, The New York Times***, and many other venues. Her interests include short lists, Oxford commas, and self-referential jokes. She peaked in 4th grade.*

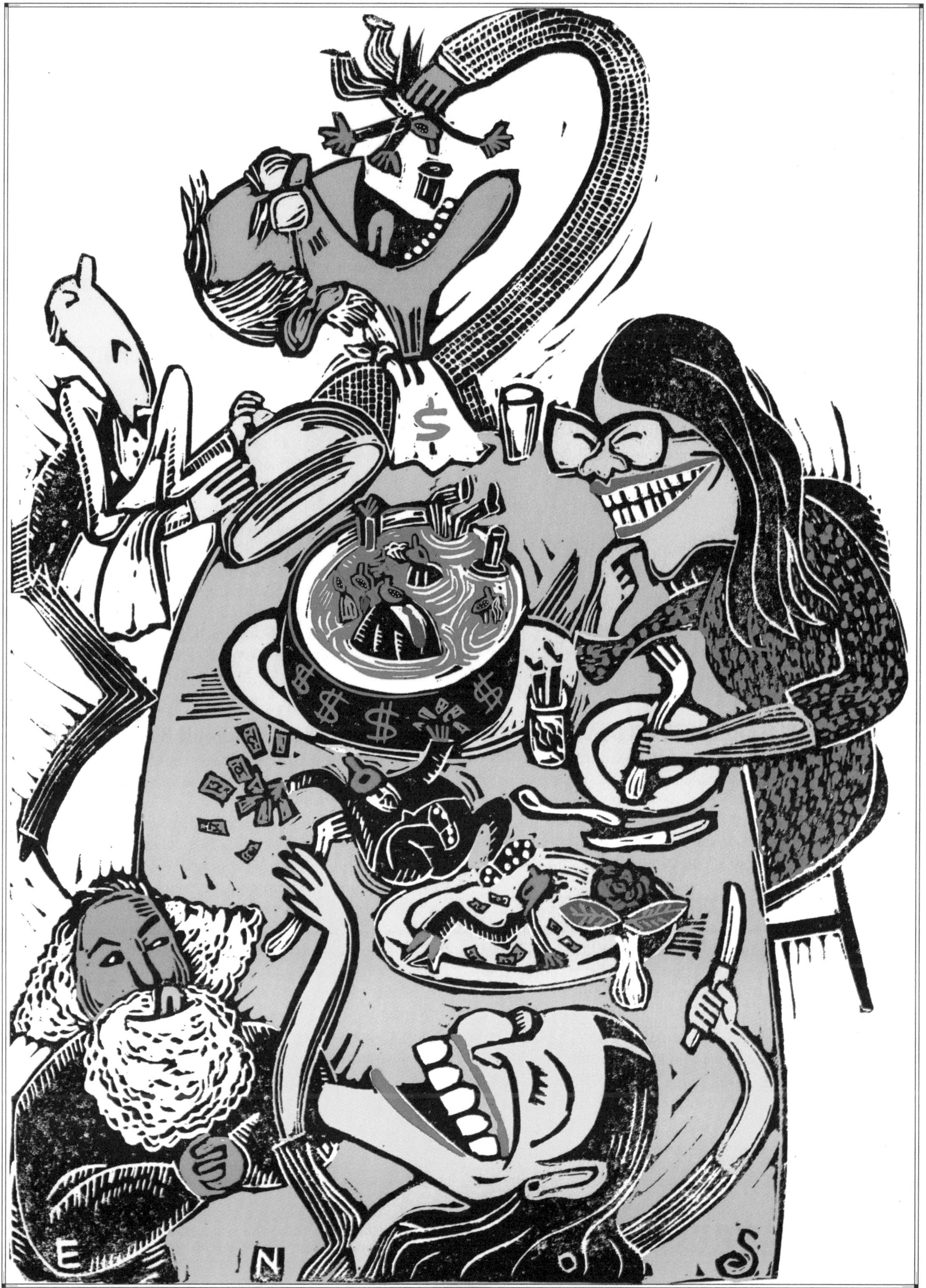
E N O S

BY MEG FAVREAU

HIRED.LY RECRUITING: FOR YOUR BUSINESS'S HUMAN FUEL NEEDS

Here at Hired.ly, we know every company is powered by *great people*—people whose joy and effort is transformed into shareholder profits by your corporate machine! But as a business owner, you don't want to waste your time searching for new employees to sink your parasitic teeth into; you want to actually do the sucking! So while other recruiting services might promise you the best employees, Hired.ly's mission is to provide you the most effective human fuel for your corporate goals.

Here's how we do it!

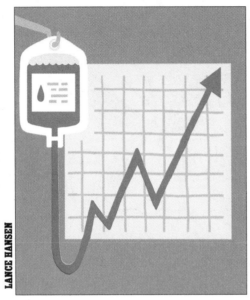

LANCE HANSEN

THE PEOPLEPIPELINE™

The Hired.ly PeoplePipeline™ is our custom employee-search algorithm. Like a pipeline for crude oil, the Hired.ly PeoplePipeline™ transports as much raw human fuel to you as possible, with total disregard for the lives it might ruin.

ROBUST RELOCATION BONUSES

Similar to how lions separate the weak from the rest of the herd in order to make their kill, we make every effort to hire you non-local candidates, separating them from their families, friends, and other social ties. With nothing left to distract them from work, Hired.ly relocation hires spend up to 47 percent more time in the office.

FOCUSING ON IN-OFFICE AMENITIES

By highlighting the fun of your free employee dinners, in-office yoga studio, and craft beer fridge, we distract employees from the fact that you'll be trapping them there long enough to desperately need all those things.

EMOTIONALLY ABUSIVE LANGUAGE

We begin the process of emotional abuse early in the recruiting process, leading your human fuel to believe that they're easily replaceable, and driving them to work harder in order to prove their basic worth. Our Emotionally Abusive Language Guide helps you continue the process, leading your human

fuel to believe that they're one mistake away from losing everything—and pushing them to work up to 33 percent harder than non-abused employees.

CHEERFUL RECRUITERS

Our cheerful, focused recruiting staff keeps every conversation positive (even while being abusive—it's an art!), so your human fuel doesn't realize that something is wrong until long after they've signed on the dotted line. How do we keep our people sounding so happy while convincing others to take soul-killing desk jobs? By practicing what we preach, of course! We even have an in-office WeepZone™ for our human fuel. The WeepZone™ is a soft room where our experts can let it all out before getting back to find you new people to burn through. Plus, we have a craft beer fridge!

AND FINALLY... A SOLUTION FOR ALL THOSE USED HUMAN HUSKS!

There's one complaint we hear time again from employers: "What do we do once we've taken everything good and right from our employees and turned them into dead-eyed shells of their former selves?" That's where our HuskHire™ Placement Program kicks in.

If you used Hired.ly for your human fuel needs, we promise to recycle your used human husks by placing them at new firm. It's a win-win situation—your dead weight will be replaced with fresh human fuel, and your spent husks will be re-employed at new firms where they'll become temporarily reinvigorated by the hope that this time might actually be different. It won't be! But they'll delude themselves into thinking it is because they'll want so badly to believe that spending forty plus hours a week for a profit-hungry megacorporation could somehow lead to a fulfilling life!

So what do you have to lose—other than profits from inefficient human fuel? Call Hired.ly today—the experts in people ruining people.   B

MEG FAVREAU *(@megfavreau) lives in Los Angeles, where she writes for animated series and regularly dresses up as a giant eye. You can see more from her at* **megfavreau.com**.

Passing for Human

Liana Finck

Dare to be Different

> "PASSING FOR HUMAN IS ONE OF THE MOST EXTRAORDINARY MEMOIRS I'VE EVER READ."
>
> — ROZ CHAST, AUTHOR OF CAN'T WE TALK ABOUT SOMETHING MORE PLEASANT?

> "NO ONE DRAWS LIKE LIANA FINCK, AND NO ONE ENCHANTS LIKE HER EITHER."
>
> — STACY SCHIFF, AUTHOR OF CLEOPATRA

A Random House Hardcover

@lianafinck 🐦 📷

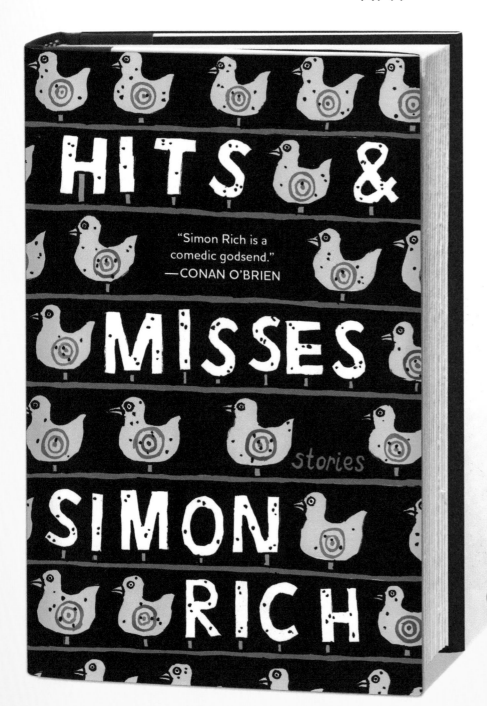

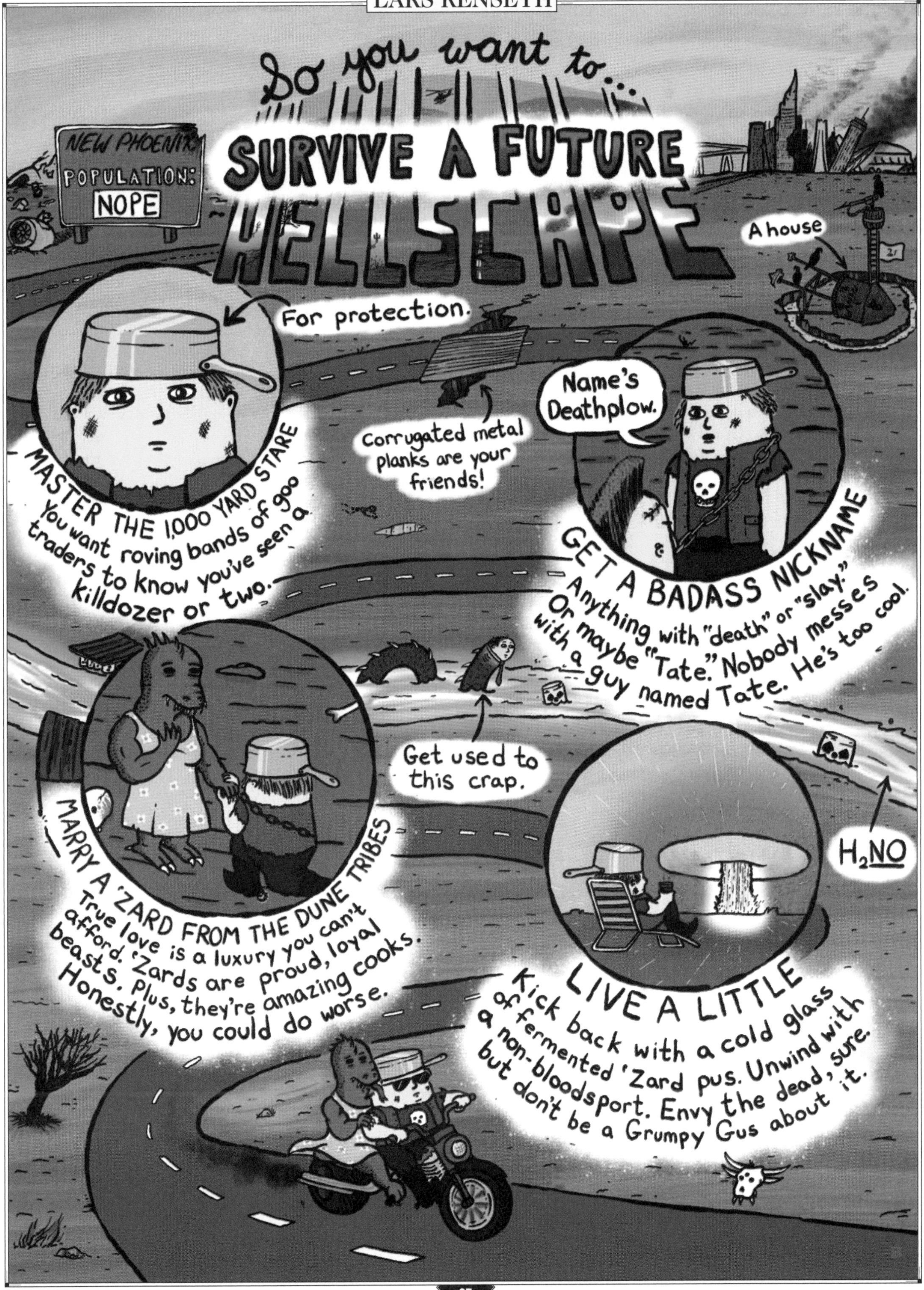
So you want to...
SURVIVE A FUTURE HELLSCAPE
NEW PHOENIX
POPULATION: NOPE
A house
For protection.
Corrugated metal planks are your friends!
MASTER THE 1,000 YARD STARE
You want roving bands of goo traders to know you've seen a killdozer or two.
Name's Deathplow.
GET A BADASS NICKNAME
Anything with "death" or "slay." Or maybe "Tate." Nobody messes with a guy named Tate. He's too cool.
Get used to this crap.
MARRY A 'ZARD FROM THE DUNE TRIBES
True love is a luxury you can't afford. 'Zards are proud, loyal beasts. Plus, they're amazing cooks. Honestly, you could do worse.
H_2NO
LIVE A LITTLE
Kick back with a cold glass of fermented 'Zard pus. Unwind with a non-bloodsport. Envy the dead, sure, but don't be a Grumpy Gus about it.

Cowboys on a Walnut Farm

Ripping through the still of daybreak, Urijah Van Zent rode in at a gallop, reined in his horse and hit the ground running. He'd thought about it enough. He wasn't going to think anymore. He aimed his heel at the bunkhouse door and kicked. It swung open, violently, hit the wall and bounced back tighter shut than before.

Some of the men sat up with a start but seeing nothing had changed, gratefully collapsed back to sleep. Except Blue-sky, who had not been asleep and for a moment saw Urijah's silhouette in the doorway and there appeared to be a gun in his hand. Blue-sky swung his feet from the bed and put on his boots.

"I didn't think he'd get it so soon," Blue-sky muttered. He thought he had another week before Urijah would return armed and with murderous intent. Blue-sky believed he had time to patch up the trouble between them. And if that didn't happen, he'd use the time to be long gone. But procrastination had always been his weakness as it was for many of the men who worked here. Where had the time gone? It was August already! Blue-sky had come to this Walnut Farm with the intention of staying a few months and saving a little money. But before he knew it, two years had slipped away. But that'll happen when you stay in one place too long. Familiarity can turn with a vengeance. Around the bunkhouse it was referred to as, "The Frustration of Misplaced Anger."

The cowboys who worked on this walnut farm had plenty of spare time. Probably too much time to overthink things. Minor things that easily inflate into brooding, important things if they weren't kept in check; if they weren't visited regularly with common sense and some humor.

The walnut cowboys considered themselves a special breed and spent a fair amount of time talking about it. They talked about who they were and why they did what they did. They talked about the pioneers who came before them and the methods they employed. They talked about the fortunes men have made speculating in walnut futures. It was a rare calling few men would confidently choose. But it was also a new era and the walnut was again, king.

Some of the men said they did it because they liked working out of doors and up in trees and bragged they could get so comfortable up there, they could even fall asleep. Others claimed it was the walnuts themselves that delighted and drew them here. How simple and intricate they were and how no two walnuts were ever alike—though the jury was still out on that popular notion. Still others found it far preferable to the more hazardous labors that might involve cattle drives, serving in the military, mining tunnels, law enforcement, open furnaces, knives, guns and hatchets. Gathering walnuts was reasonably safe and steady work. But to a man, they all liked the bunk time that went with it. Awake by 9, most of them didn't roll out of the sack till around 10:30. It also gave them lots of time to read. The walnuts weren't going anywhere. And those who did get an early jump on the job, were usually beat by early afternoon and spent the rest of their day asleep in trees or back in their bunks reading or napping a chunk of the day away or talking to one another about the pleasures and mysteries of this life, as well as the motives they had for choosing this work.

Some of the men worked in pairs; one upon the other's shoulders. Sometimes even in threes; the man, or men, above picking the walnuts and the man below, the strength, holding forth the bushel baskets catching the walnuts. Some, like Blue-sky, preferred to go solo. With a sack on his back, he'd climb a walnut tree and shimmy out on a limb. Still others, the ones with excellent balance, the ones who owned horses and guns, would stand atop the horse's saddle and tap, tap, tap the walnuts loose with the butts of their empty pistols. And for those fearful of heights, there were usually enough walnuts on the ground to satisfy their quota if they knew where to look (which wasn't always that obvious). One thing they all hoped to do was spot a sacred walnut. A walnut that might miraculously contain a miniature depiction from the Bible: Lot's wife being turned into salt; or Moses delivering the plagues upon Egypt; or Jesus carving a wooden box in which to store fish. These walnuts could fetch a lordly sum if they were in good condition and the image was arguably clear.

Brian McConnachie *is Co-founder and Head Writer of this magazine.*

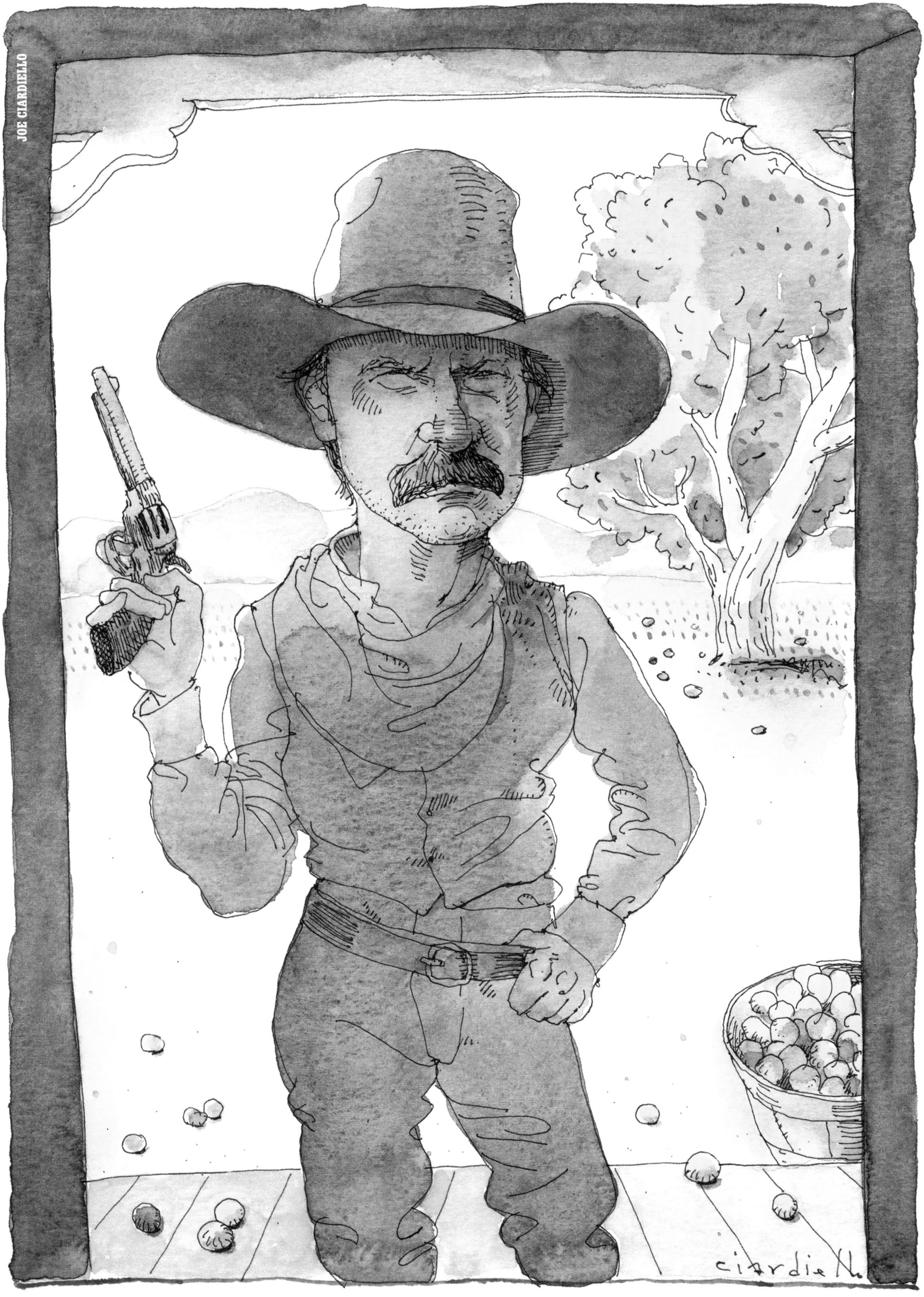
JOE CIARDIELLO
ciardiello

"Make it look like nine accidents."

The door flew open again, and Urijah caught it as it came back at him. This time more of the men awoke, and they knew Urijah had gotten the money he needed to purchase a bullet and now would be the reckoning. They sat up in their bunks, fluffed their pillows and got comfortable.

Yes, Blue-sky realized, Urijah had a gun in his hand and as importantly, the bullet to go in it.

The nearest town that sold weapons and reliable ammunition was Tilman, some fifty-five miles away. There, the cost of a bullet—the round, the casing and the powder—came to about $48. Guns, they practically gave away. For the cowboys who worked on a walnut farm, this was a substantial sum to acquire; the decision to shoot someone with a bullet that expensive was a commitment not entered into lightly. The last shooting occurred more than four years ago, and no one now present was witness to what actually happened. One of the versions, however, was they each shot the other in their walnut-gathering hand, rendering each other unfit for this profession they were so suited to and loved. Both separately departed for other labors, leaving behind their cautionary tale.

More recently, there was a fight, but not with guns. The participants agreed it would be restricted to kicking, biting,

nose- and ear-twisting, and punching. It also included, for a while, whacking each other over the head with smallish, tightly packed, burlap gift bags of fresh walnuts which the Troys, the owners, were test-marketing at the time and were being stored everywhere in abundance. The noise it made sounded far worse than the slight damage it inflicted. These two men, both considered to be "talkers," detested each other and disagreed on most everything. Their original conflict was, "Who actually said 'an unexamined life is not worth living,' Socrates or Plato?" Then the premise, "the unexamined life," became separated and wandered off, only to later reappear as a conundrum-provoking, "How unexamined can a life actually become?" The battle didn't include as much ear- and face-biting as some of the cowboys would have wished, but neither participant wanted their mouths to be occupied when they could be logically advancing the arguments each so tenaciously championed. In spite of the enthusiastic pounding the combatants gave and took, the battle raged for almost an hour. It was finally abandoned when both men, beaten into exhaustion, had to be carried to their bunks, where they were confined for several days and where each spent a fair part of that time, cursing the other and, in spite of the pain of bruised ribs, feebly tossed books at each other's heads.

Most of the men assumed that this fight, about to unfold before them, was over the affections of Dolores Troy, the daughter of Big Jake Troy, the owner of the eight-hundred-acre Oh So-Lazy-Oh Walnut Farm & Ranch-Oh.

Dolores Troy and her father lived in a fourteen-room, yellow Victorian farmhouse that was constructed with the promise that one day it would be filled with Big Jake's grandchildren. It sat centered in the circular shade of five oaks and one walnut tree, and stood about a quarter of a mile from the bunkhouse and mess hall. Dolores was a serious, efficient and oddly handsome woman in her mid-30s who rarely smiled but possessed a kind nature. She tended to the farm's business. She was tall but well coordinated, and could navigate a walnut tree as well as any man or maybe any primate. She weighed the walnuts, paid the men every Thursday evening (as they in turn tried to see down her blouse). She also kept from her father all offers—each more generous than the last—from manufacturers, worldwide, who wanted to haul off a large percentage of the walnut trees and make pianos out of them. Dolores's deceased mother, though declaring to enjoy music, in fact detested every piece of music she had ever heard, and made Dolores swear on a Bible she would never do anything that would remotely benefit the music industry.

It was also Dolores who interviewed new men for the job. She sometimes conducted these interviews on the upper limbs of the oak trees. Both Blue-sky and Urijah showed confidence ascending the trees and returning safely to the ground, which spoke well for them both.

"Why did you leave your last job?" she asked.

Blue-sky said he'd been a bugler in the United States Cavalry. Speaking on behalf of the other buglers, he complained to his commanding officer that, in addition to chipped teeth and split lips from the ever-elusive mouthpiece, the buglers found it nearly impossible to produce a sequence of notes on such a small musical instrument while bouncing about all herky-jerky on the back of a galloping horse over rugged terrain and be expected to play anything remotely recognizable as "Charge!" or "Retreat!" or "Go Left, Everybody."

"I don't know anything about any small musical instruments," Dolores suddenly interrupted, almost ending the interview—but when she was assured that he no longer played the bugle (especially on horseback or any other conveyance) she gave him the job. Then asked him to hurry down and send up the next candidate, Urijah.

Urijah told her this would be his first job. He was right out of college. He didn't speak much and had small interest in music.

Urijah, who slept up top, and Blue-sky below, had been bunkmates for as long as both had been there. They arrived at the ranch on the same day. Lying around as much as the walnut cowboys did, a few became skilled storytellers and speakers, while others developed as listeners and thoughtful, inquisitive, editors. For the most part it sorted itself out that the talkers bunked with the listeners.

Urijah grew into a talker, and Blue-sky initially appeared to be a most enlightened listener.

But when Urijah arrived he was far from being a talker; he was painfully shy and kept to himself. He was also distrusting. He ate alone. He avoided eye contact. He moved quickly past people, as if he expected they would slap the back of his neck to hurry him along; to hurry him out of their sight. If someone nearby suddenly raised a hand in gesture, Urijah was prone to flinch. At night, on occasion, he would scream in his sleep—but in this behavior, he was not alone. There were nights in the bunkhouse when the place sounded like a crazed zoo with half the men having nightmares, usually involving falling. On other nights could be added men leaping from their bunks trying to escape the sudden pain of leg cramps, and then colliding into one another as they hopped around in the dark.

Several of the men came to believe that Urijah Van Zent was shouldering a dramatic weight as he looked around for the right, deep enough hole to drop it into. Or person to leave it with. But until that happened, if ever, he'd not be fit company. He was judged as having

too many demons to be working in such a tranquil place as a walnut farm.

"What is your name and where are you from?" Blue-sky asked him.

Urijah's response was barely audible. Aware of the man's shyness, Blue-sky didn't inquire further. He would, however, nod when he'd catch Urijah's eye. Gradually Urijah grew relaxed in Blue-sky's presence; he found Blue-sky comforting.

Some months later, the fellow in the next bottom bunk, Tyrel—a fellow Urijah suspected of having neck-slapping potential—got out of his bed and sat on the floor next to Blue-sky's bunk.

"May I speak with you?" said Tyrel.

Blue-sky nodded. "Yes. You may."

"I was lying in my bunk the other morning and thinking about the natural order of things. I realized we all have enemies. When we meet them we usually know it right off. And we can do little about it. Like that fight over Plato and Socrates a while ago. They were just fighting, it didn't matter about what. That was no, "Frustration of Misplaced Anger"—those two hate each other. Have you thought about this? Is there some eternal element, something I'm not considering while trying to understand why we naturally have enemies? Who are they and where do they come from?" Tyrel asked Blue-sky. "Why do we have enemies, and could the answer to this, in part, explain war?"

Blue-sky was silent with his thoughts.

"I will think about this," he said.

"Thank you. I appreciate it," said Tyrel.

From his bunk, Urijah listened and agreed with the man's quandary, but was also without resolution. But he was impressed that his bunkmate was held in such high regard as to be entrusted with a question of this magnitude.

Several days passed, and Urijah was lying on his bunk, reading and dozing, when Blue-sky returned from his day's labors. He'd been sleeping in trees the last two nights. He went to Tyrel's bunk. Tyrel was asleep, and Blue-sky shook his foot. The man awoke. Blue-sky stretched out on his own bed before speaking.

"Maybe our enemies are family members from past lives," Blue-sky said.

Urijah, hearing this, slapped a hand over his mouth and uttered, "Oh my God!" into it.

Propelled, Urijah jumped down and knelt by the side of Blue-sky's bunk. Knelt by the side of this wise man's bed and spoke urgently after months of silence.

"*Yes!* That's exactly who they are! It makes perfect sense. That's it, right there," Urijah began. "I have family in St. Louis. A big family. I left home. I was the only one who left. They're all still there. I don't know why they stay together. They all hate each other. This isn't past lives. This is going on right now," said Urijah. "But, yes! That's where our enemies come from. I see

"I have no inner life."

that clearly. Our own families are the seeds of it. Who knows us better and can do us more harm? How did you come to know this?"

Blue-sky shrugged. But from then on, Urijah Van Zent began to find his voice as well as the person he felt compelled to share it with.

He randomly began with stories of his family's behavior. He had never before done this. It had been drilled into him that behavior inside the family was no one else's business. It was a large family. There was a lot to keep quiet about. Urijah felt the importance of breaking the silence. Of bringing forth a number of experiences to share with Blue-sky. He started with the time his mother forced his youngest sister, then age 5, to eat an entire Vidalia onion because the child failed to tell her Mommy how much she loved her. Then there was an aunt, on his father's side, who had a penchant for wandering the house, late at night, slapping other relatives across the face while they slept—to pay them back for a slight, real or imagined, that may have occurred earlier that day or even years before or never.

Urijah's family confessions were usually done in the morning, before the day's walnut gathering began. He would sit on the floor at the side of Blue-sky's bed, and speak in a volume only Blue-sky was meant to hear. Each session, before he spoke, Uriah's instinct directed him to respectfully ask, "May I speak with you?"

Blue-sky would traditionally reply, "Yes, speak with me."

Over the next weeks and months, Blue-sky heard stories of cruelty, revenge and neglect, all emanating from the twisted core of the Van Zent household. The volume of this family's contemptible behavior was beginning to appear endless. But with Blue-sky now seeming to share this burden, the dramatic weight began lifting from Urijah. Urijah's nature was becoming renewed, showing self-confidence and friendliness. He nodded to his co-workers. Occasionally, and with some delicately, he patted their backs and wished them well on their day's gatherings. Some of the men found this awkwardness annoying, but it was an improvement over the sullen Urijah—and most of the cowboys found it hopeful to witness that such change is possible.

For a while, when Urijah collected his pay, he made sure he was last in line so he could have some time to speak with Dolores Troy (as well as look down her blouse). He greeted her with his biggest smile. He would ask her about the business. No one had shown this interest before, at least not to her, and she had plenty to report on the subject. She told him they were developing a hybrid walnut shell. It was more weather resistant and yet, easier to open. The plan was, she told him confidentially, to bring it to market next spring. It should be ready by then.

"Dad believes we'll be the chief beneficiary of this—but he also thinks it will be good for the entire industry," she said. "It'll get more people saying, 'Have you heard what's been going on with

new King Walnut?' And isn't that what we all want to know? Will King Walnut be getting into the same special bag as cashews and pistachios, yea or nay?"

Then one morning, on a notable occasion, Urijah did not ask, "May I speak with you?" If he had, Blue-sky most probably would have replied, "No! No more," and put an end to this.

But neither happened, and Blue-sky's politeness was again subjected to the latest oppressive installment of the Van Zent chronicles.

"Now I'm going to tell you something really terrible. Are you ready for this?" Urijah began, "The holidays we all spent together..."

On more than a few occasions, cowboys pulled Blue-sky aside or climbed an adjacent tree and asked him, "What does Urijah say to you every morning?"

"I can't listen anymore," Blue-sky said. "I don't hear him after two sentences. But he never stops. Whatever he's saying, it's always awful, one bad thing after the next. The tone of his voice tells me how to react, and I make appropriate sounds in response," said Blue-sky.

"Be careful of him." Blue-sky was warned more than once. "Urijah's not really a walnut man. When a listener ignores a talker...well, you know what they say..."

"I'll be fine," Blue-sky would reply.

Late one Thursday evening, Blue-sky and Tyrel were discussing the changing value of industriousness over bravery in a world trying to become more civilized, (or was it?) when Urijah entered the bunkhouse talking out loud to himself. He sat on Blue-sky's bunk and continued speaking.

"...do you know where I've been? Do you know why I'm so late? I thought she'd never shut up. Yap yap yap about the walnuts. The walnuts this and the walnuts that. And then, who knows, maybe she'll build a house out of walnuts. Make shoes out of walnuts. Sure, why not? Then I have to swear to God I won't tell anybody, especially the men who work on the adjacent walnut farms, what we've got going on here. Otherwise, we might be looking at an out-and-out range war. 'And nobody wants that.' And, oh! By the way, we're all going to have to start signing, 'non-disclosure agreements.' Whatever those are."

As he spoke, Urijah saw Blue-sky's eyes shut—and he began nodding and humming in much the same fashion as when hearing the Van Zent calamities. Could it be possible Blue-sky wasn't listening, thought Urijah? Or could it be he just wasn't listening to this latest barrage of walnut claptrap?

To test him, Urijah asked in a mirthful tone, "Blue-sky, do you remember when I told you about that Christmas Father gave Mother a silk-lined box with a snake in it?"

Blue-sky responded with a warm reminiscent hum.

"And do you remember the time my one normal uncle who everyone thought was a lunatic took me on a wonderful holiday to Chicago?" he asked in a voice trying to be dense with pain.

Blue-sky sighed a condolence.

Urijah went to bed that night believing it wasn't possible that Blue-sky hadn't been listening; hadn't been sharing this huge burden. But that night, sleep would not come to Urijah. It wasn't till after daylight that he finally dozed off.

When Urijah awoke, later that morning, the bunkhouse was empty. His breathing was doglike, quick and shallow; he was having an experience he had not before known. He lay still as this reality gripped him deeper and squeezed him tighter. He understood—but didn't know how he understood—that from then on, he alone was responsible for all the internal functions of his own body. All those parts he knew or didn't know or had once heard mentioned: carotid artery, optic nerves, bone marrow, the liver and pancreas. Whatever, or whoever had effectively been in charge of running everything in sequence, or in unison or in balance was no longer present on the job. This once-automatic arrangement had unexplainably ended. A thought told him he had been alive long enough to now know how it all worked and to keep it working. And if he didn't, it was no one's fault but his own; he should have payed better attention. So he was now alone to manage his thalamus and kidneys and immune

system and lungs and bone marrow and those many extra yards of different-size intestines. The whole caboodle. All he knew was, the brain sent out signals and the rest obeyed. But he had nothing to tell his brain that would achieve this. "Digest the meal I ate and keep my heart beating," was not going to be specific enough for this new arrangement. But if it were possible to give the correct directions, would his brain even obey? Could the soul maybe jump in here and on occasion outrank the brain, and get things back on track? It would show some real character. But there was great risk in this. There was a lot that could go wrong. There is probably an entire chapter on keeping the appendix from suddenly rupturing and even more on not mixing up the blood flow with the body's waste. The simple truth remained, Urijah knew nothing. But if he didn't learn something soon, these would be the final moments of his short, tortured, misspent life. He'd stop breathing. For a moment he paused in his terror to curse his family for not sending him to medical school, then returned to his dilemma. Maybe he could find an ally like the pituitary gland, whatever that was. Or enlist enzymes, whatever they were, and get them on his side. In turn, maybe they could get their working colleagues to come over to his side. But this was risky, considering he'd be starting from nothing.

The grip on his chest tightened. He

crossed his arms upon his chest in a fatal pose and shut his eyes, waiting for the inevitable as he grew helpless and angrier at this happening to him.

Urijah Van Zent took the bullet from his pocket, waved it teasingly, then put it in the chamber. Blue-sky moved to the side and began climbing over bunks heading towards the back wall. Urijah followed.

"Get away!" "Out in the middle!" "Fight over there!" "Don't you come near here with that gun!" ordered the men who were being climbed over.

"You'll be picking walnuts this day in Hell with the Devil," said Urijah to Blue-sky, ignoring the cowboys' yells.

"They pick *coal,* not walnuts, ya dope," a voice corrected.

"That's why it's Hell," another voice offered.

"Did you listen to *any* of it?"

"Yes!" said Blue-sky, continuing to back away.

"Then," demanded Urijah, "what happened to my grandmother during Christmas dinner that time?"

"She choked on a bone!"

"No!"

"No one would listen to her!"

"NO!"

"She dropped dead and no one stopped eating!"

"Actually, that's pretty close..." said Urijah. "But you're guessing."

"I'm warning you, Urijah, don't shoot."

"I used to be miserable. I was happy then."

Windowless and doorless, the back wall put an end to Blue-sky's retreat. He brought up his arms to protect his head, then slid down the wall drawing his knees tight to him, trying to become as small an object as possible.

"Hey Blue-sky!" someone yelled. "Can you see into the abyss? What's it like?"

Urijah took careful aim.

Everyone flinched at the report of the gun.

If Blue-sky had been posing for a life-size depiction of Christ's crucifixion, and Urijah had been allowed to bring the gun as close as three feet, he still would have missed by an embarrassing margin.

Blue-sky slowly unfolded himself. He got to his hands and knees and crawled back to his bunk.

Urijah looked at the gun in disbelief: How did *that* happen? He held it by the trigger guard away from him as if it were contaminated.

The men started jeering and laughing and kicking their blankets in the air.

With unconvincing jollity, Urijah asked: "Bet you thought you were a goner, huh? Ha, ha! I had you going, didn't I? Oh, did I tell you what Dolores said about the new walnut hybrid? It's actually kind of interesting..."

Blue-sky emptied the money from his secret pouch and started counting it on the bed.

"What do you think, Blue-sky, how long?" asked Tyrel from his bunk.

"Two weeks! Maybe a week and a half if I put in extra walnut time," said Blue-sky.

"Is that counting the time to Tilman and back?"

Urijah didn't know if he should run for it or keep changing the subject until he hit on something truly engaging. **B**

D. WATSON

Agony Comics

Indulge your inner sadist by watching other people suffer!

SIR, I REGRET TO INFORM YOU THAT YOUR ENTIRE FAMILY HAS JUST PERISHED IN A FIRE! I'M SURE YOU'LL WANT TO KNOW THAT YOUR FATHER'S LAST WORDS WERE "ARRGHHHHHH!"

I'M SORRY, BUT THE ELECTRIC CHAIR ISN'T WORKING TODAY! WE'LL HAVE TO SIT YOU BETWEEN TWO SHORTED-OUT TOASTERS!

THIS IS THE LOCAL ASPCA! DID YOUR DOG HAVE A HABIT OF SITTING ON RAILROAD TRACKS?

I'M SORRY, BUT THE PATHOGEN LEVEL IN YOUR BODY HAS REACHED THE CRITICAL AMOUNT! IF YOU HAD GOTTEN HERE JUST FIVE MINUTES EARLIER, WE COULD HAVE SAVED YOU!

I'LL MAKE A DEAL WITH YOU! I WON'T EVICT YOU IF I CAN SELL YOUR CHILDREN AS SLAVES!

I HOPE IT WILL BRING YOU SOME SMALL COMFORT TO KNOW THAT THE TIGER REALLY SEEMED TO ENJOY THE TASTE OF YOUR HUSBAND!

I'M AFRAID WE'RE GOING TO HAVE TO AMPUTATE EVERY PART OF YOUR BODY EXCEPT FOR YOUR LEFT FOOT!

I NOW PRONOUNCE YOU FUTURE DIVORCEES! AND BITTER ONES!

APART FROM DOOMING YOU TO TOTAL STARVATION, THE SWARM OF LOCUSTS HAS BITTEN THROUGH YOUR TV CABLE!

DOCTOR, HOW MUCH TIME DO I HAVE LEFT?

I'M SURPRISED YOU WERE EVEN ABLE TO FINISH THAT SENTENCE!

I'M AFRAID YOUR 17 CHILDREN HAVE BEEN ABDUCTED BY 17 DIFFERENT KIDNAPPERS, EACH DEMANDING TEN MILLION DOLLARS IN RANSOM!

AND TODAY I LOST MY JOB DOWN AT THE FACTORY!

DARLING, IF YOU BREAK UP WITH ME, THEN I'LL COMMIT SUICIDE! BUT IF YOU DON'T BREAK UP WITH ME, I'LL KILL YOU!

THERE'S AN EXCRUCIATINGLY PAINFUL TREATMENT THAT MIGHT EXTEND YOUR LIFE UNTIL TOMORROW AFTERNOON!

WOULD YOU PREFER TO HEAR BAD NEWS ABOUT YOUR SON FIRST? YOUR DAUGHTER FIRST? OR YOUR CAR FIRST?

I'M SORRY TO TELL YOU THAT THE KIDNEY TRANSPLANT FAILED! SO DID THE LIVER TRANSPLANT, THE LUNG TRANSPLANT, AND THE HEART TRANSPLANT!

YOU HAVE SIX DREADED DISEASES, EACH OF WHICH CAUSES UNBEARABLE PAIN! ALSO, YOU THREW UP ALL OVER YOUR INSURANCE POLICY, MAKING IT UNREADABLE!

WHY ARE YOU SO SILENT, DOCTOR?

MY PARENTS ALWAYS TAUGHT ME, IF YOU DON'T HAVE ANYTHING NICE TO SAY, DON'T SAY ANYTHING AT ALL!

AT FIRST WE THOUGHT ONLY THE EARTH WAS GOING TO BE DESTROYED...THEN WE REALIZED IT WAS THE SOLAR SYSTEM TOO...ALSO OUR GALAXY...AND OUR CLUSTER OF GALAXIES...AND THE UNIVERSE...AND THE ENTIRE MULTIVERSE!

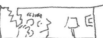

B

FIGURE HAIKU

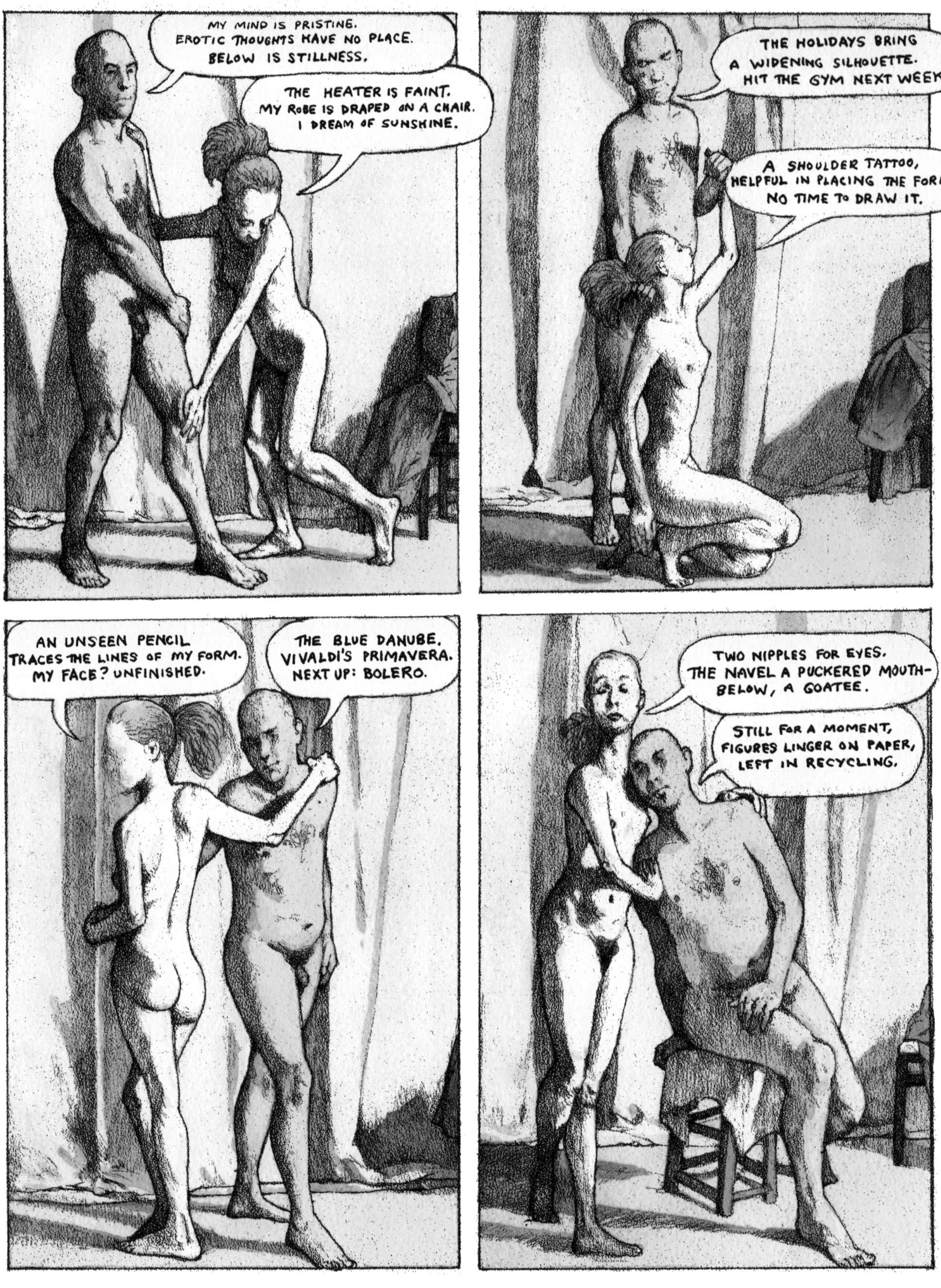
MY MIND IS PRISTINE. EROTIC THOUGHTS HAVE NO PLACE. BELOW IS STILLNESS.
THE HEATER IS FAINT. MY ROBE IS DRAPED ON A CHAIR. I DREAM OF SUNSHINE.
THE HOLIDAYS BRING A WIDENING SILHOUETTE. HIT THE GYM NEXT WEEK.
A SHOULDER TATTOO, HELPFUL IN PLACING THE FORMS, NO TIME TO DRAW IT.
AN UNSEEN PENCIL TRACES THE LINES OF MY FORM. MY FACE? UNFINISHED.
THE BLUE DANUBE. VIVALDI'S PRIMAVERA. NEXT UP: BOLERO.
TWO NIPPLES FOR EYES. THE NAVEL A PUCKERED MOUTH- BELOW, A GOATEE.
STILL FOR A MOMENT, FIGURES LINGER ON PAPER, LEFT IN RECYCLING.

B

The Nixon File

Found: one political career,
slightly soiled.

When I was a kid growing up in Orefield, Pennsylvania, I used to work on my father's garbage truck. Every weekend, holiday, or school break between the ages of 15 to 22, I would get up in the morning-dark and accompany Dad on his route, helping him gather up the garbage and throw it into the truck. Then we'd haul it to the dump.

It was, to be frank, a great gig. In the summertime, when I'm out biking around New York City, I sometimes end up parked behind a garbage truck at a red light. While the drivers around me are gagging or covering their noses, I'm caught up in a wave of sweet nostalgia. Proust had his madeleine...

Why did I love it? Because people throw away all sorts of good stuff. For one thing, I got lots of records: James Brown, the Rolling Stones, Motown, jazz, country, classical, soundtracks, comedy, oldies. I was introduced to a lot of music that way, stuff that I never would've heard otherwise. I'd listen to all of it. For obvious reasons, I was particularly partial to "Surfin' Bird" by the Trashmen.

The file cabinet in question, February 2019.

It's not a stretch to say that my time as a junior garbageman actually changed my life. The drawing table I work on to this day came from the trash.

Each week, someone on the route would throw out their copy of *New York* magazine. I remember sitting in the truck reading about New York artists—Chris Burden having himself nailed to a Volkswagen, Vito Acconce masturbating under a bridge—and thinking, "I really want to live there." My mother said I started talking about moving to NYC when I was 6 years old. My parents were supportive. My father's only piece of advice was given to me while we were on the truck. He said, "I don't care what you do with your life, just don't do this shit."

One of our daily stops was *The Allentown Call-Chronicle* newspaper. This was always a favorite; not only were there often cool books and magazines in their trash, there were no wet coffee grounds, wilted lettuce or rats in it. (Nothing like a rat jumping out of the garbage can you're dumping to wake you up in the morning.) Sometime after Richard Nixon resigned in August 1974, somebody at the paper hauled out the disgraced president's wirephoto file, and dumped it into the trash. Clearly, *The Call-Chronicle* wouldn't have Dick Nixon to kick around anymore; after Watergate, nobody would.

Not surprisingly, I took this archive home with me. My father used to say that when I worked with him there would always be more stuff in the cab —things that I collected along the route—than there was in the back of the truck. This was a slight exaggeration but only slight. And I pretty much still have the best of what I collected back then. The only thing that got away, also Nixon-related, was a box of Nixon campaign flasher buttons that I left on the truck one day and my dad threw them in the dump.

Back then the area was staunchly union and Democratic, so there was no love for Tricky Dick. I used to draw lots of anti-Nixon cartoons on the cardboard shirtbacks one of the department stores threw away. I gave a lot of them to a girl I knew, after my mother threatened to throw them out. Sadly, that romance didn't last, and those shirtbacks ended up back in the trash.

Anyway, this file has remained with me for forty-five years, for one simple reason: I never throw anything away.

Why am I telling all this now? Why am I moved to share photos of a man who was, for a time, the most powerful person in the world, ending up in the trash?

Oh, no reason.

···········◆···········

Stephen Kroninger's *work can be found in the permanent collections of the Museum of Modern Art, the Library of Congress, and the National Portrait Gallery in Washington.*

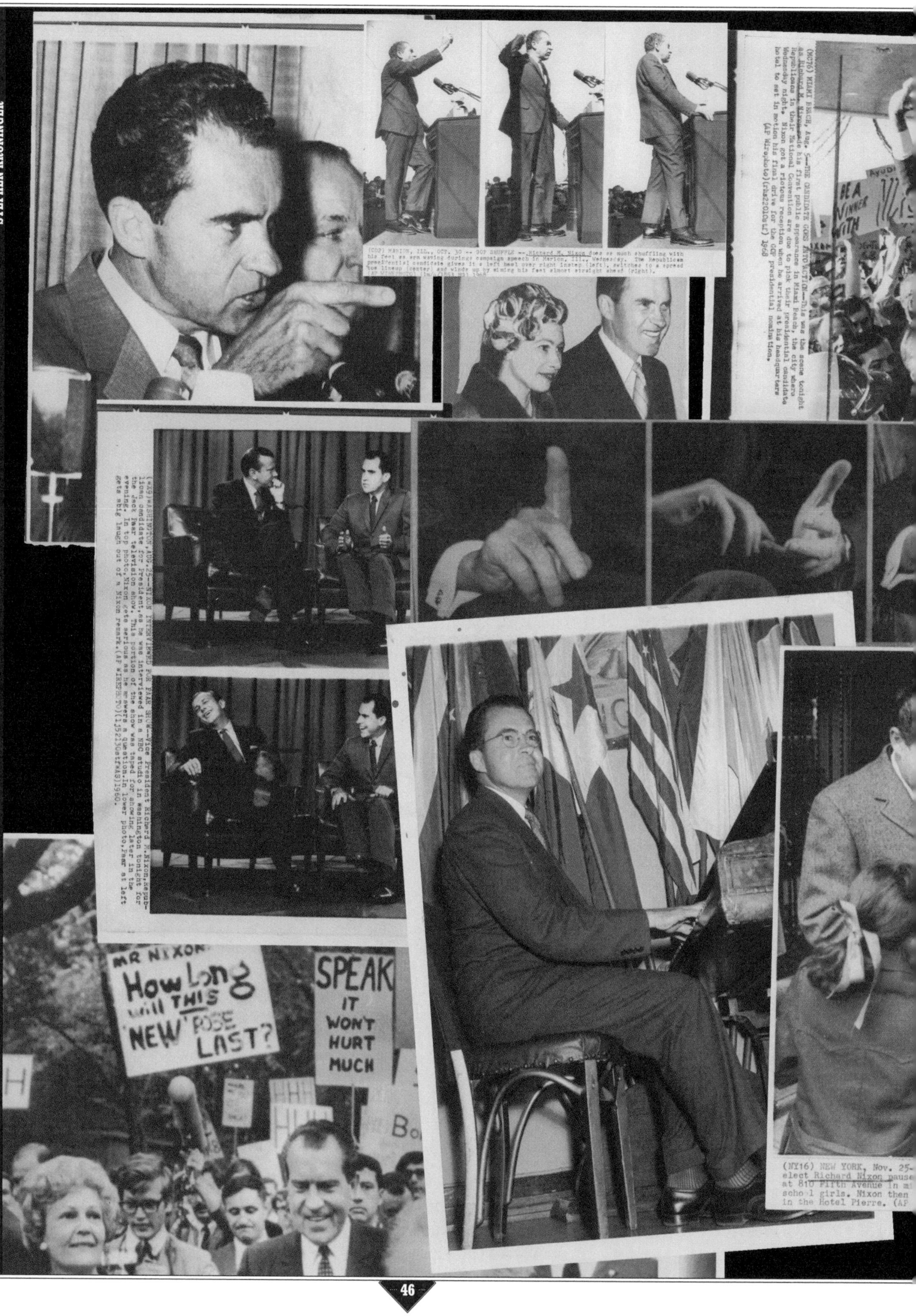
(CD2) MARION, ILL., OCT. 30 -- GOP SHUFFLE -- Richard M. Nixon does as much shuffling with his feet as arm waving during campaign speech in Marion, Ill., Wednesday. The Republican presidential candidate gives it a left heel over right instep (left), switches to a spread toe lineup (center) and winds up by aiming his feet almost straight ahead (right).
MR NIXON
How Long will THIS NEW ROBE LAST?
SPEAK IT WON'T HURT MUCH
(NY16) NEW YORK, Nov. 25-
elect Richard Nixon paus
at 810 Fifth Avenue in m
scho l girls. Nixon then
in the Hotel Pierre. (AP

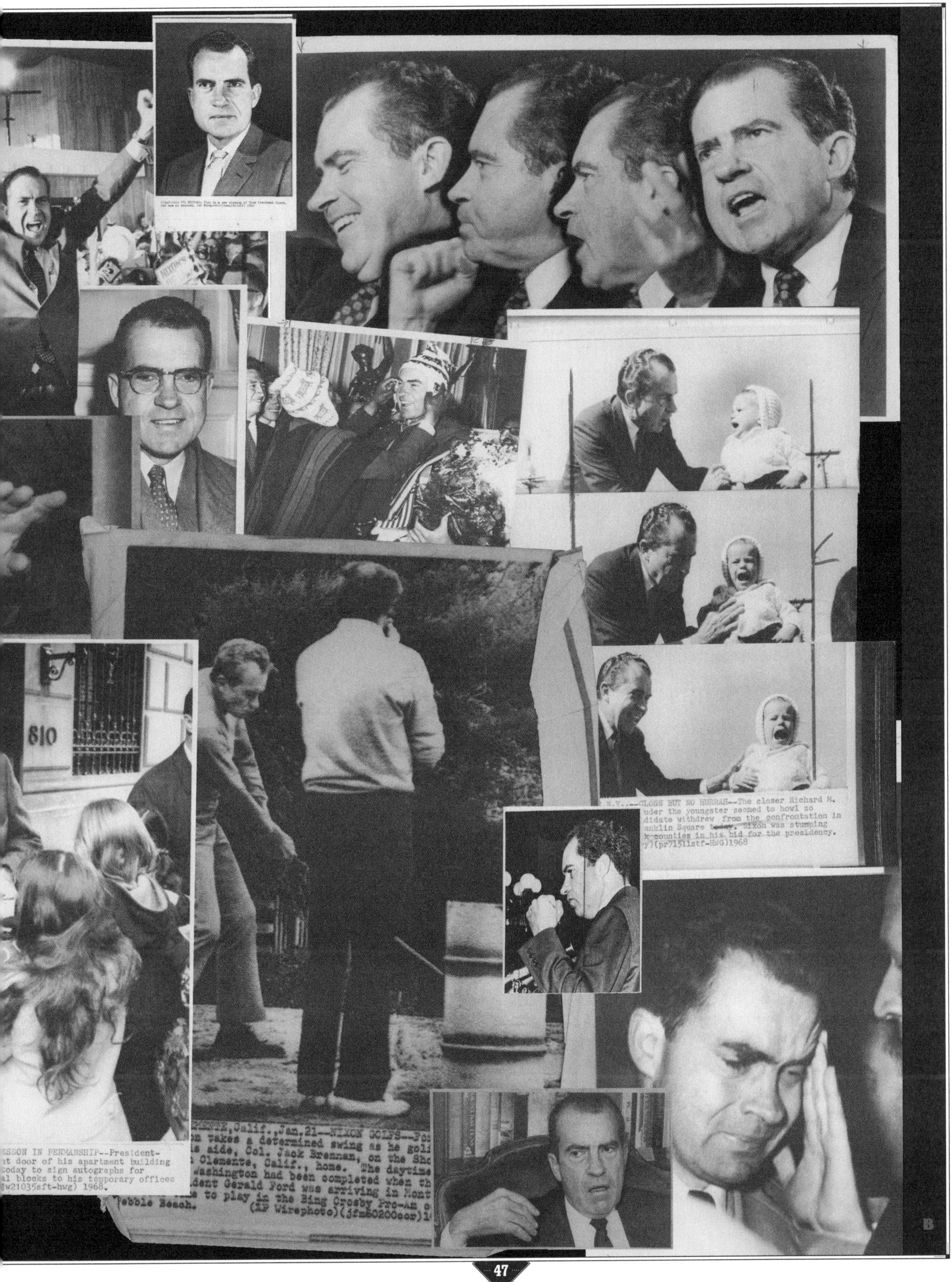

810
N.Y...--CLOSE BUT NO HURRAH--The closer Richard M.
uder the youngster seemed to howl so
didate withdrew from the confrontation in
anklin Square today. Nixon was stumping
k counties in his bid for the presidency.
y)(pr71511stf-HWG)1968
ESSON IN PENMANSHIP--President-
nt door of his apartment building
today to sign autographs for
al blocks to his temporary offices
(w21035sft-hwg) 1968.
ENTE, Calif., Jan. 21--NIXON GOLFS--For
on takes a determined swing as he golf
is aide, Col. Jack Brennan, on the Sho
n Clemente, Calif., home. The daytime
Washington had been completed when th
dent Gerald Ford was arriving in Mont
to play in the Bing Crosby Pro-Am o
Pebble Beach.
(AP Wirephoto)(jfm80200cor)1

A Dream of Consequence

Tales of The American Bystander, *1981*

John Belushi tossed me in the air.

In memory, I soar a good twenty feet over his head, as if I have been launched in some coked-out version of the Eskimo Blanket Toss. At the apogee of my flight, I can see Brian's brownstone, there on the south side of 78th Street. I can see the American Museum of Natural History just a couple blocks away. I can even see the scary building uptown where I live in with my roommate, a young film-maker named Charlie Kaufman. And there down below, on the sidewalk, are the McConnnachies, Brian and Ann, and the Belushis, John and Judy. The lights of New York City shine all around.

It's spring of 1981. I'm 23 years old, a closeted trans woman, the managing editor of *American Bystander* magazine.

I descend. Belushi catches me in his arms and lowers me to the sidewalk. "See ya," he says, and he and his wife step into a waiting cab.

I walk up the steps into Brian's house. "Belushi just threw me up in the air and caught me," I say, a little bit stunned.

"You're lucky," says Brian. "He doesn't catch everybody."

I'd moved to New York on Veterans Day the autumn before, bearing with me a small backpack, a book by Neal Cassady, and an autoharp upon which I was pretty sure that in days to come I'd be singing ironic coal-mining songs in coffeehouses. It wasn't that I didn't understand that the days of folk music had come to an end about twenty years earlier. But I figured I'd be turning all that around, what with my own insufferable genius. I settled into an uptown apartment with Charlie, where he edited a film in his bedroom and I sat at a desk in the foyer, working on a novel called *Ammonia Quintet*.

The story concerned a wizard named Fezriddle who owns an enchanted waffle iron that keeps attacking him with its hot mouth and wagging its electric cord tail behind like a Siamese cat.

He sings a little song to the waffle iron:

The man in the moon says, "Please keep it down."
The churchbells are waking up the dead.
A fool looks better than a headless clown.
Send yourself to bed.

The only way the wizard could stop the attack was to pour batter into the waffle iron's mouth, where it sizzled and smoked until the waffles were ready. How did he know when the waffles were ready?

When the steaming stopped.

To underwrite this enterprise I got a job working in a bookstore called Classics. It was just a couple doors down from Radio City, on 48th and Sixth. We had to wear name tags bearing the store's logo, but we were warned by the store's manager not to use our real names, because people had been known to look clerks up in the phone book and call them up and breathe. As my tag-name, I chose "BOPPO."

I spent my days at a booth located in the center of the store, doing inventory control. I sat beneath a giant sign that said, "Ask Me Anything." I usually started each working day doing a couple bongs uptown before taking the 1 train down to Classics. By the time I got myself into position, I was ready to be asked anything.

"Excuse me, Boppo," said one customer, frustrated that the bookstore contained only books. "Where are all the Santa Claus suits?"

☛

----- ◆ -----

Jennifer Finney Boylan is Anna Quindlen Writer-in-Residence at Barnard College. Author of 15 books, she's a Contributing Opinion Writer for *The New York Times*. In 1981, she was Managing Editor of *The American Bystander*.

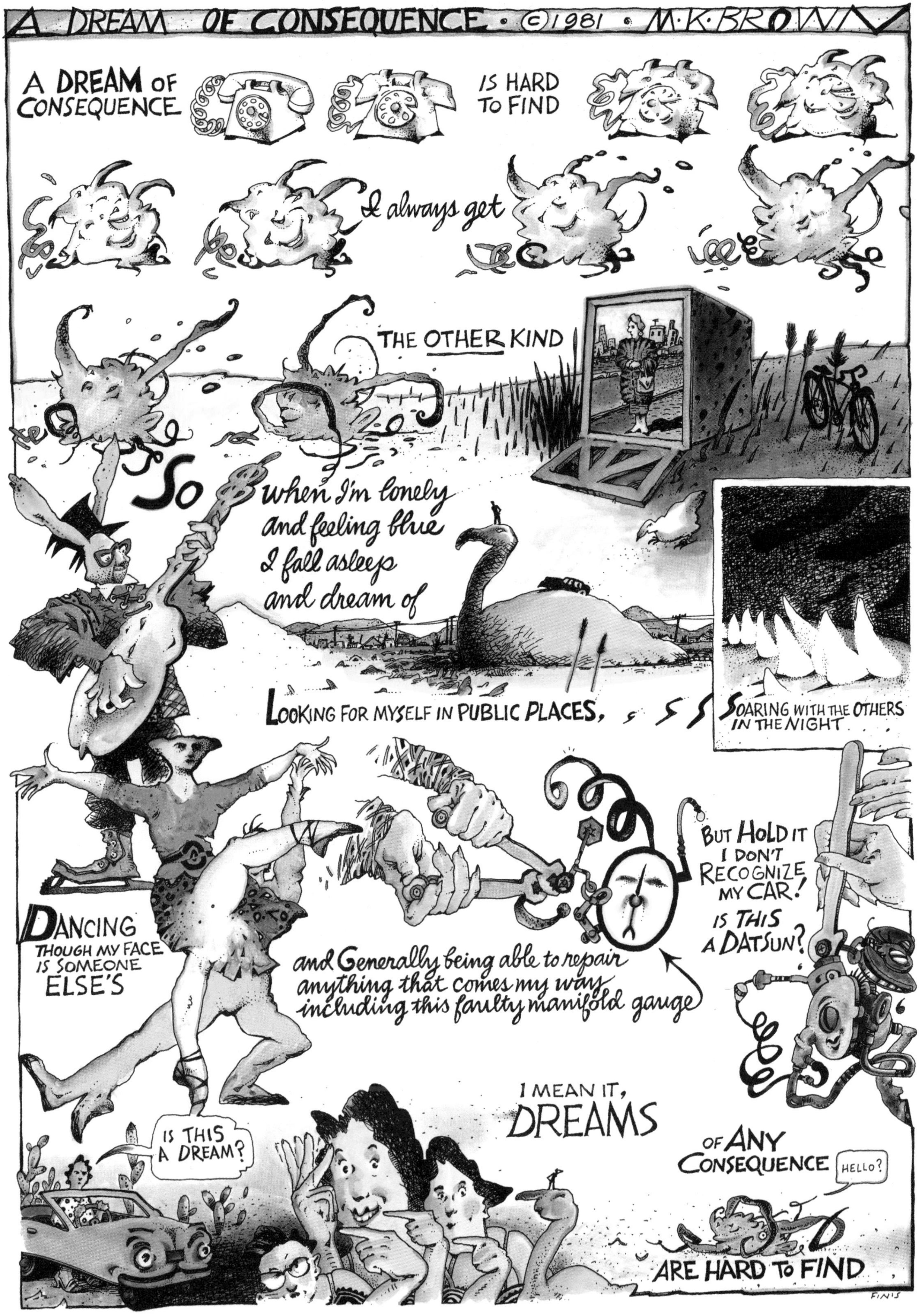
A DREAM OF CONSEQUENCE • ©1981 • M.K.BROWN
A DREAM OF CONSEQUENCE
IS HARD TO FIND
I always get
THE OTHER KIND
SO
when I'm lonely and feeling blue I fall asleep and dream of
LOOKING FOR MYSELF IN PUBLIC PLACES,
SOARING WITH THE OTHERS IN THE NIGHT
BUT HOLD IT I DON'T RECOGNIZE MY CAR! IS THIS A DATSUN?
DANCING THOUGH MY FACE IS SOMEONE ELSE'S
and Generally being able to repair anything that comes my way including this faulty manifold gauge
I MEAN IT, DREAMS
IS THIS A DREAM?
OF ANY CONSEQUENCE
HELLO?
ARE HARD TO FIND

The author (right) at The Bystander's publication party in 1982. Behind Boylan, Brian (left) talks to the writer Bill Franzen. (Photos by Doug Kirby)

My mother, back in Pennsylvania, played bridge once a month with a nice group of ladies, one of whom allowed as how her son George was the publisher of a new humor magazine. Mom got the name and phone number of the son, and gave it to me. I wrote the information down on the waxy cover of a box of Entenmann's coffee cake. There it sat for a month or two, until I finally got the nerve to call a man whose name was George Dillehay.

"Think of *The Bystander* as a grown-up *Lampoon*," he said. It was being assembled by a group of writers, co-medians, and artists who had recently left *Saturday Night Live*, including Dan Aykroyd, Belushi, Gilda Radner, Bill Murray, and Lorne Michaels—as well as some folks from *SCTV*, Dave Thomas and Rick Moranis and Harold Ramis. A few *New Yorker* cartoonists were involved, too—including Jack Zeigler, Mick Stevens, and Roz Chast.

The editor-in-chief was one Brian McConnachie. Brian's not a household name, then or now, but he should be. He'd been an editor at *The National Lampoon* in the 1970s; he'd written for *SCTV* as well as *SNL*. His humor was hard to define, but is perhaps best summed up by a sketch he wrote, "Vikings and Beekeepers." A summary on YouTube describes it thus:

"The Vikings, tired of the routine of sacking England, attempt to torment the English even more by bringing over bees. But the voyage proves difficult as the beekeepers insist the bees may only travel East at night. There's a theme song as well, which goes to the tune of Wagner's "Ride of the Valkyries," and whose lyrics are, 'Vikings and Bee-keepers, Vikings and Bee-keepers, Vikings and Bee-keepers, Vikings and Bees!'"

George Dillehay gave me Brian's phone number. I called him up. Brian sounded kind, gentle, and amused. He said: "I'm glad you called. I've been looking for an aide-de-camp."

He invited me over to the offices, and we made an appointment to meet.

In those days I was clutching on to mas-culinity in a manner not completely unlike Bugs Bunny walking off of a cliff into thin air, prevented from falling only because he has not yet realized there is no firm ground beneath him. In 1981, the whole idea of being out as trans seemed preposterous. Embarking upon transition, I felt, surely would only result in ruin, in scandal, in public mortification and probable violence. It would mean I would lose every relationship I had ever had, that I would be disowned by my parents, and that I would never be loved by another soul, ever. It would mean that instead of understanding and com-passion I would become an object of ridicule, marginalization, and disgust.

Thank goodness everything has completely changed since then and that trans people never have to worry about people reacting like that when they find the courage to reveal their unexpected truths. Ha! Ha! Ha! Ha! Ha! Ha! Ha! Ha! Ha! Ha! Ha! Ha! Ha! Ha! Ha! Ha! Ha! Ha! Ha! Ha! Ha! Ha! Ha! Ha! Ha! Ha! Ha! Ha! Ha! Ha! Ha! Ha! Ha! Ha!

And so, wearing a gentleman's coat and tie, I headed over to *The Bystander*'s offices, which turned out not to be offices at all, but a brownstone on the Upper West Side. Brian's wife, Ann, answered the door. She seemed a little uncertain. I explained who I was, and she said, "Well, Brian's not here."

She probably would have shown me out except that I looked so crushed, standing there in my ill-fitting Oxford shirt. I had, since my conversation with Brian, invented quite an alluring fantasy about what *The American Bystander* might become. At the very least it would get me out of Classics Bookshop.

Ann showed me up to the attic floor of the brownstone, where there was a small

Roz Chast chats with Ed Subitzky, with Judy Jacklin Belushi in the back-ground. In the foreground, cartoonists Bill Woodman and Bob Mankoff.

office with a desk and a piano and lots of books. She told me I could wait there until Brian returned, although she didn't know exactly when this would be.

I sat in a chair for a while, wondering whether I should just head home. On one wall was the original of a cartoon about Brian in *The Lampoon*'s "Self Indulgence Issue." The piece was called "Brinie," drawn in the style of "Blondie." The premise of the cartoon was that Brian was dead, and all the other *Lampoon* writers had gathered around for the funeral. In one panel, Michael O'Donoghue asks, "What kind of wine goes best with grief?"

After a while, I sat down at the piano and began to noodle around—the McCoy Tyner version of "My Favorite Things." It was a long jam in E minor. I must have played for twenty minutes, just goofing around, seeing where the ideas would go.

When I finally stopped playing, a voice behind me said, "That's really good."

I turned around, and there was Brian McConnachie, a tall, handsome, slightly bewildered-looking man whose glasses magnified the size of his eyeballs slightly. He'd slipped in while I was playing, and just sat there listening.

"Mr. McConnachie," I said, getting to my feet.

"Yes, very good," he said, almost to himself. "Visceral. Well. You're hired."

"I am—? What do you need me to—?"

"We'll work it out as we go along," he said, ushering me down the stairs.

Before I knew it, I was back on the street outside.

I would work for *The American Bystander* for the next two years—the title we finally chose for me was "Managing Editor," which was very funny, since Brian could neither be edited nor managed.

When people ask me how I got the job as an editor, though I can only tell them the truth: I was the only pianist who applied for the job.

THE AMERICAN
BYSTANDER

1982

Views of the Passing Parade

$2.00

Religion Sex and Politics.

Money, Love and Death.

Dreams and Encounters.

Sport, Space and Crime.

Beauty and Art and Bugs.

Short Stories.

Color Comics.

High Ideals & Common Sense

PILOT ISSUE

The original idea was this: to create a general interest magazine that would appeal to the generation that had read *The National Lampoon* in their teens and twenties. You might think there'd have been an abundance of such magazines in 1981, but you'd be wrong. *The New Yorker* had been publishing the same magazine for fifty years. Other general interest publications aimed at prior generations—*LOOK*, and *Life*, and *The Saturday Evening Post*—had shriveled or died.

In 1981, it would be another decade and a half before the internet posed its mortal threat to the magazine industry. There was a brief moment when it seemed possible that a newer generation, raised on 'zines and underground comics and

The Lampoon, might find its voice in print. Art Spiegelman had launched *RAW* magazine in 1980. At Conde Nast, plans were being hatched to reboot *Vanity Fair*, dead since 1936. It would be four years before Kurt Andersen and Graydon Carter launched *SPY*, and eleven years before Tina Brown brought *The New Yorker*, kicking and screaming, into the future. There was plenty of energy in the air for something new, and a hole in the market—could *The American Bystander* fit into it? We thought so.

Of course, it's logical to wonder why the new *National Lampoon* wasn't, you know, *The National Lampoon*. In addi-

51

NOW IT CAN BE TOLD

For over 30 years, The American Bystander languished as one of the great "what ifs" of the comedy business. It seemed like a can't-miss idea: a new humor magazine created by one of the main editors of The National Lampoon, featuring his friends from Saturday Night Live and SCTV, with investors like John Belushi and Lorne Michaels. In 1982, if anybody had the guts— and good will—to make a new national humor magazine happen, it was Brian McConnachie. But after producing a proof-of-concept for advertisers and newsstand people, the project lost momentum. I'd always wanted to find out exactly what had happened, so as I edited Jenny's piece, I called Brian and asked him a few leading questions.

MG: What gave you the idea?
BMc: It must've been 1975 or '76 — I was still at **The Lampoon**, not yet at *SNL*. The author Richard Price came to me with these stories, and I remember thinking, "These are really good, and funny, but they're outside our idiom." I realized how limited a palette we were working with there, as great as it was, and started pondering something a little different.
MG: Is Jenny right in remembering it as a hip *New Yorker*, or grown-up *Lampoon*?
BMc: As far as I'd thought it out at that point. I wanted it to be where you went after you aged out of **The Lampoon**. And I wanted the art to look great. I wanted a magazine that was at least as big as your head. With apologies to B. Kliban…But what magazines are, they become in the making—the pilot issue was my initial sense,

cont. on p.54

tion to the brain-drain which siphoned the original staff (Brian included) to greener pastures like *SNL*, that magazine faced a knotty conundrum. As Brian explained it to us, the choice was "whether to grow up with its readers, or to remain focused primarily on its current audience of adolescent boys." At some point, *The Lampoon* decided to stay put. People other than me can argue about whether that was a good choice—but for *The Bystander*, the way seemed clear.

On February 28, 1982, *The New York Times* ran one of its periodic laments about the sorry state of print humor. But sandwiched among the gloom was this hopeful note: "Two new publications in the planning stage, *The American Bystander* and *Vanity Fair*, intend to run humor alongside news features, panel cartoons, photo layouts and poetry, in the classic—and perhaps now antiquated—general-interest magazine style… Brian McConnachie says, 'There is so much young talent around with no place to show their work. The readers have just gone away. They haven't died." But it was another thing Brian that said which explained why *The Bystander* thrilled me to the core. "Magazines are one of the last places that can risk failure," he said. "Noble failures, where you see all the rough edges, are terrific. You learn more from noble failures than you do from slick successes."

By the way, over at *The Bystander*, we rolled our eyes at the prospects of *Vanity Fair*. Oh yeah sure, we said. Like *that'll* ever come out.

But what they had, and we lacked, was what Harold Ross had had back in 1925—a benefactor. *The Bystander* needed someone like Raoul Fleischmann, the yeast magnate.

Brian had enormous good will in the comedy world, having been the only person to have pulled off the '70s Comedy Trifeca: *The National Lampoon, SCTV*, and *SNL*. But good will was not the same as owning your own yeast factory, and it's possible that the love of all of his friends—most of them now becoming famous and wealthy in Hollywood—was not enough to sustain a long-term business venture.

We were funny, we were creative, we were young. But yeastless, we were doomed from the start.

There were so many close calls. We took meetings with venture capitalists. We attempted to woo a member of the oil-rich Schlumberger family. Once, I spent an afternoon with some of the publishers of Marvel Comics. Everyone was curious, and interested to see what the future might hold.

But no one wrote a check.

There were really two teams on the creative front—one was the old *Lampoon* and *SNL* crew, a group of people nearing the age of 40, old hands at all of this, many of whom contributed work primarily out of love and respect for Brian. The other was the group of young and hungry that I spearheaded, most of us having graduated from college sometime around 1980. This junior cohort was a goofy group of people, containing many souls who later went on to have careers of their own. In time, Bruce Handy toiled for both *SPY* and *Vanity Fair*. Trey Ellis wrote the screenplay for *The Tuskegee Airmen*, then became a professor at Columbia. Chris Van Allsburg, who contributed a full-color cartoon to the pilot issue, later wrote *The Polar Express*. Mimi Pond and Liza Donnelly have gone on to fine careers as cartoonists. All in all, a mighty impressive group, and an enviable collection of young talent.

But back then, it was a lot like chaos. Because *The Bystander* did not yet exist, it was hard to articulate exactly what it was going to be. And the only person who could rule definitively on this was Brian McConnachie. Who was, as I said earlier, a tremendously generous and affable man. But who was more than a little vague sometimes, in part because I think he didn't want to hurt anyone's feelings by simply telling them no, and in part because he wasn't entirely *sure* of anything.

Looking back, it might be that Brian's soft focus, his lack of a hard, cruel edge doomed us, too—after all, a magazine really does need someone to be the bastard. Brian didn't want the magazine to be overly political, or quite frankly, to have many opinions at all, besides the wistful observation that the world is pretty goofy. Our pilot issue had "Views of the Passing Parade" on its cover, by way of explanation of what was inside.

That issue contained plenty of funny and interesting things. But even our biggest fans had to agree that views of the passing parade seemed like a less edgy vision of the world than—well, say, the *Lampoon* cover with someone holding a gun next to the head of an adorable dog.

I ran *The Bystander* for the summer of 1981, while Brian was in Canada filming *Strange Brew*, Dave Thomas and Rick Moranis's movie about the beer-swilling McKenzie brothers. When he returned, in the fall, we moved into offices at 444 Park Avenue South, subletting the space from a printing company that published, among other titles, *Working Woman*. There was a small chamber where Brian sat at a desk looking out the window, and a larger room—the "bullpen"—where the rest of us worked. As I said earlier, Brian had anointed me the Managing Editor, and Bill Woodman, a veteran of *The New Yorker*, was Comics Editor. Bill's ex-wife Barbara Shelley was the Art Editor. Louise Gikow, from *The Lampoon*, was copy editor and dispenser of common sense. And Brian's childhood friend Peter Dews was News Editor.

At the end of each day, we would repair to a Blarney Stone, where we would drink beer and Peter would secretly pick everyone's pockets. At the end of a session, he would point to the bar, where all of our things were arranged in a pile.

Another regular gathering spot was Beacon Lanes, the bowling alley on Amsterdam. We sat at the bar at the back of the room and watched everyone bowling. One time, Billy Murray joined us, and rolled strike after strike. The woman behind the bar was the same person who rented you the bowling shoes. Later, as she drew a bunch of pints from the tap, she told me that someone from Hollywood had been through recently, and offered her a million dollars to shut the place down for a month while they shot some movie.

"Well?" I asked. "Are you going to do it?"

"Nah," she said. "We thought about it. But then we figured, it would only screw

up the leagues."

This was the kind of story we'd write about in *The Bystander*. It was literally happening all around us, and no one was paying any attention.

A friend called me at *The Bystander* one day, and Peter answered the phone. "No, he can't talk right now," he said. "He's out bystanding."

Later, she wondered—bystanding? What on earth was this?

It was a question that I myself had difficulty answering, not that I didn't attempt, mightily, to find out. One day, I interviewed a woman who ran something

.... ◆ ....

I know it never actually happened. But just because it never happened doesn't mean I can't remember it.

.... ◆ ....

called the Skunk Club, a kind of support group for people in Manhattan who kept skunks as pets. She was an angry woman with black hair pulled back in a tight bun. "People shouldn't have skunks," she told me, practically yelling. "They don't make good pets!"

Through her I found out about a couple who ran a monkey orphanage out on Long Island. I went out there with a photographer. To my horror and amazement and fascination, the husband was transgender. "You just have to accept yourself," said she.

Right, I thought. As if.

On another occasion I rode around in a UPS truck all day. A week later, I took a ferry out to Hart Island, the potter's field of New York City, where the homeless are buried in long rows by orange-jumpsuited prisoners from Rikers. (I didn't know it at the time, but my grandfather's bones lay there

at my feet.)

I spent an afternoon with the members of the Titanic Society in a bar. After a few rounds, they started to sing: *It was sad, when that great ship went down.*

There were a couple stories Brian was working on, but never seemed to finish. One of them was fiction, a story entitled "Cowboys on a Walnut Farm." The other was titled "Joan's Other Kitchen." We weren't sure exactly what this was about. Every idea we came up with seemed, somehow, less wonderful than that weird, hilarious title.

Then there was the day we decided to float cartoonist Roz Chast across the Gowanus Canal with weather balloons. One of the young writers consulted with a physicist, figuring out exactly how many balloons it would take to levitate her. It would take a lot of balloons, he concluded, but we could do it.

All systems were go with this caper—until Roz found out about it. "Listen," she said. "There's no way I'm doing that."

When I recall my *Bystander* days, I picture Roz Chast, a small, nervous woman, slowly becoming airborne, floating like Icarus above the aromatic waters of the Gowanus Canal.

I know it never actually happened. But just because it never happened doesn't mean I can't remember it.

The pilot issue of *The Bystander* was published in the summer of 1982. A group of us took a road trip to the printers in New Haven. We rode in a convertible—a Mustang, I think—with the mechanicals and the page proofs in the trunk. The wind blew our hair around, and we listened to rock 'n' roll music on the radio. It was me and Brian and Barbara Shelley. Cartoonist Mick Stevens was there, too. We handed all our stuff over to the printers with great fanfare and then cheered loudly and after that we were on our way to the legendary Sally's for pizza.

Then we headed back to New York.

It'd be a couple weeks before the issue came off the press. In the meantime, we but it would've refined itself as we did issues.

MG: Who did you have working with you on the publishing side?

BMc: I had met a fellow named George Dillehay, a publishing guy with an MBA. So when I got serious about making a run at it —after *SNL* and *SCTV*—I asked George if he'd help us out. He did for a while, but I think he saw the writing on the wall and jumped fairly quickly to *The **Village Voice**,*

MG: Why was it so difficult? I remember there was a recession right then, the Reagan Recession.

BMc: For all the things we had going for us, our timing was bad, and so much of this stuff is in the timing. And I think the culture had already moved beyond magazines—that wasn't where the juice was, anymore. I remember going into some guy's office at one of the big newsstand distributors —

MG: Cue *The Godfather* theme.

BMc: —this real handsome guy, and I was just so determined. I laid it out there for him, just poured my guts out for about 15 minutes. But he wouldn't budge. A new humor magazine in 1982? He wasn't buying it. I kept telling him the numbers, and he finally said, "Look. You seem like a nice guy. But I don't care if it makes me a million dollars a day and gets me a blow job every afternoon, I'm not going to do it."

MG: That's weird. If you've got the cash, guys like that—

BMc: I think that was it. He knew we didn't have the cash. Not that I didn't try. I tried for a year to raise money. After the guy at Independent News turned me down, I went to see these two lesbians, really tough ladies who would take your trucks and smash your kiosk if you didn't pay tribute.

MG: Shades of Moe Annenberg!

BMc: Investors were even crazier. I remember a guy— I met him at a party or something— who ran an illegal gambling den down in the garment district. All the *schmatte* merchants would come in after

all turned, for the first time, toward the unsettling process of figuring out what was going to happen next.

Oddly, or inevitably, what happened next was nothing.

People started moving on. One of the young writers, Mike Wilkins, left New York to get his MBA. Another got a job at an accounting firm. A third did a series of interviews with the older *Lampoon* luminaries; when he sat down with Michael O'Donoghue—whose poem "Bears" graced the pilot—he mentioned *The Bystander.*

Mr. Mike said, "Everyone knows that thing's never coming out."

One day, comedian Harry Shearer came into the office. What's the story, he wanted to know.

"We are in a dark tunnel," I replied. "But we're going over the top."

The first copies of the pilot issue arrived in midsummer, and it was a sweet, startling work of art. There was a short story called "Death 'n Dennis," and a science feature on space junk, and a sports piece on spelunking. In lieu of letters to the editor, there was a page where people mailed us an account of their dreams.

Mr. Mike's poem was called "Bears."

A wizard blew an Eskimo way down to Egypt-land;

He found he had no word for snow, and they no word for sand.

For years and years they searched to find the thing that each man shares,

And in the end, to their surprise, they found that thing was bears.

Not glossy, but on stiff, white paper, *The Bystander* was broadsheet-sized, both taller and broader than *The Lampoon* or *New Yorker*, and the art looked great. Our well of beautiful full-color comics included a surreal piece by M.K. Brown called "A Dream of Consequence." An illustrated dreamscape, the first panel contained this couplet: *"A dream of consequence is hard to find. I always get the other kind."*

I spent part of that summer housesitting for my parents in Pennsylvania, where I shaved my legs for the first time and one night sat by an open window watching a furious thunderstorm. A bolt of lightning struck a pine tree twenty feet from the house. I watched the electricity fork from the treetop to the roots.

The house shook upon its foundation.

Later, I went out west with my friend Peter, where I walked along the beach at the Olympic National Seashore in Washington State, feeling darker and darker, understanding with each passing mile exactly how impossible the life I needed to live would be. One day, as we walked by the ocean, I met an Ozette Indian, who pointed overhead and said, "There's an eagle," and there it was, soaring overhead in wide circles.

I told him I hadn't seen it before because I was looking at the ground. "If you only look at the ground," he said, "you'll never see the eagle."

I asked him what his job was, and he just smiled wanly. "I control the tides," he said.

When I got back to New York, I had the strong sense that it was time to move on. I got a job at Viking Penguin as an assistant to the managing editor. I went into the *Bystander* office one day to take my leave of Brian. We shook hands.

What kind of wine goes best with grief?

I moved to Maine in 1988 to take a teaching job at Colby College. Ten years after that, with the support of my wife, I slowly began transition. There were times when I thought it might cost me my job, my children, my life. But somehow we all survived—and even thrived. A decade or so later, I had three new jobs—one as writer-in-residence at Barnard College of Columbia University, one as contributing opinion writer at *The New York Times*, and one as the chair of the board of the LGBTQ human rights organization, GLAAD.

Now this, I thought, as I unexpectedly found myself back in New York again, living not ten blocks from the scary apartment I had once occupied with Charlie Kaufman, this is a dream of consequence.

One day, I read in *The Times* that *The American Bystander* magazine had reemerged. Editor & Publisher Michael Gerber wrote, "This is willfully re-launching the Titanic, knowing full well it will sink."

I wrote Gerber a little letter, introducing myself as the Managing Editor of the pilot back in 1982. I told him a few stories of the Auld Days—about the monkey orphanage, about riding around in UPS trucks, about the day John Belushi had thrown me in the air. Gerber replied with generosity and kindness, and even invited me to a little party *The Bystander*'s third partner, Alan Goldberg, was throwing to celebrate the publication of a recent issue.

And so it was that thirty-five years after lightning struck my mother's pine tree, thirty-five years after the Indian pointed up at the sky to show me the eagle—after all those years, one day I walked through the doors of a bar on the Upper West Side to meet the staff of *The American Bystander*.

There was cartoonist George Booth, sitting at a table with Sam Gross. There was Roz Chast, who did not regret for one second her refusal three decades earlier to be floated across the Gowanus Canal by weather balloons.

And there was Michael Gerber himself, who welcomed me with enthusiastic grace.

I felt a little bit like the old knight at the end of *Indiana Jones and the Last Crusade*, after guarding the Holy Grail for 2,000 years. I wanted to say, "I knew that you would come."

Brian McConnachie wasn't there, though. These days, he's in Florida— God knows he's earned it. I asked Michael if he'd told my old boss about my transition, and how the author of "Cowboys on a Walnut Farm" had taken the news of my metamorphosis.

Michael said that news of my transfiguration had brought my old boss only joy. Yes, very good. Visceral.

A couple of copies of the new magazine lay upon a table. It contained stories, cartoons, full-color comics, some fiction. There was even a column by Brian entitled "Joan's Other Kitchen." It had taken over 30 years, but he'd finally figured out what this was all about.

I remembered M.K. Brown's comic from the pilot issue. A dream of consequence is hard to find. I always get the other kind.

W hen I got back from my trip out west in 1982, I picked up my pilot issue of *The Bystander* for the first time, and spent an afternoon looking at it in wonder. I had a date with a girl named Kate that same evening, and I showed her the magazine. Later, I played her some ironic coal-mining songs on my autoharp.

We walked out into the New York night, ate some dinner at a Chinese place. Afterwards we sat on a bench overlooking Riverside Park, in front of the very building that I would live in forty years in the future. The skies grew dark, and it began to softly rain.

I put my arm around her, and we kissed. We thought about going back inside, what with the storm, but instead we just sat there a little longer, she and I, feeling the rain upon our faces. **B**

work, shoot craps or play 21, and lose tons of money. Anyway, he got this bright idea. "I'll tell you what we'll do, Brian. We'll throw a 'Vegas Night' at the Plaza Hotel, someplace swanky. You'll invite all your movie star friends, and we'll rake in plenty. Just gimme half."

There was a business guy who really seemed to want to help, but he wasn't liquid enough. I was getting up to go when he said, "Hold on. I need to make a phone call." The guy then proceeded to phone his stockbroker, and very slowly explain a buy order he wanted the broker to place for him at the beginning of trading tomorrow. As he talked, every so often he would look at me like, 'Are you getting this?' He was giving me a hot stock tip. And it was a good one! But I couldn't do it; it felt like gambling. This was all my friends' money, which I gave back when *Bystander* didn't happen.

The closest we got was this big cocaine dealer. He said, "I've got $2 million in this desk." I don't know how much it was, but it was a drawerful!

MG: What did you say? Do you still have his number?

BMc: I said, "Let me talk to my partners." I went to a business guy I knew and asked, "If I take this money, how likely is it that I'll end up in prison?" He said, "Very." So I had to turn it down.

MG: I have to ask: Did you ever approach Matty Simmons?

BMc: Matty was interested in other things by then. He'd bought a bank in Beverly Hills with all the money he'd made from *Animal House*. I didn't want to do it—the whole *Lampoon* thing had left a bad taste for all of us. But as a last resort, I went to see him. I remember, before I went off to the meeting, I found my daughter —she was a toddler then—and I hugged her and said, "I'm doing this for you, darling."

But Matty had moved on. And eventually I did, too. **B**

...AND TODAY: *Jenny Boylan (right) and friend. (Photo by Deirdre Finney Boylan.)*

The Tiny Taxi of Justice

A Rex Koko, Private Clown Mystery.

Down here in Top Town, everyone's got a beef. When kinkers are with a show, performing and traveling and making a living, they're the happiest, most generous people you'll ever meet. But when they wash out and end up stuck here, hustling quarters from the townies every night in the same dingy yard, the glamour of the circus dims quick.

So it's always hard to lose one of the good ones — and Tillie was one of the good ones. Not just her act, though she was one of the greatest flange artists you'd ever see. But she also had a kind heart for everyone she met, including yours truly, Top Town's Least Popular Joey.

A flange act, for you elmers out there, is an aerial acrobatic act. The aerialist slips her hand into a loop of silken rope, is lifted into the air, then begins to twist and swing her body vertically 'til she's doing circles, heels over head, like a windmill. One of the hardest things you can do to your body; dislocates your shoulder at every rotation. Tillie's record in flanges was 75.

It's a shame she had to go and marry that greasy Rollo. Then, two weeks ago, in the middle of her act, she had the accident. Only no one believed it was an accident.

Tillie heading south like that left us all under a cloud. It never lifted even after the funeral. She had reminded all of us of that one person in our past who stuck with us, no matter the weather. And then she, like them, went the way of all flesh. And after that, there was nothing left around Top Town's sagging, weather-beaten flash but more flesh.

Speaking of flesh, there was no better place to see it than the Club Bimbo, one of our top cooch shows with the best dames and skimpiest costumes around. One day, before the Businessman's Lunch matinee, I brought a pack of smokes to the owner to see if a little chat could cheer me up. But my old pally Lotta Mudflaps was hanging crepe as bad as me.

"Ah don't know what it is, Rex," Lotta said as we smoked by the stage door. "Ah didn't know Tillie all that well, but that pore lil thing, ending like that . . ." The former "World's Daintiest Fat Lady" brushed away a tear.

"I hear ya," I said, feeling a little humid myself. "People fall from their rigging once in a while, but somehow, I thought she could float down and land on her feet. Like a little bluebird."

"Yew were sweet on her, weren't yew?" she teased, nudging me and sending me sprawling.

"Hard not to be," I said, dusting myself off, "with how she helped get that big molasses can off my head. That was a clambake to remember... Ya know what makes this worse? Rollo."

"Now, Rex, don't get started . . ."

"The shifty bum," I snarled, leaning my foot on a bucket. "He had somethin' to do with it, I'd bet the farm on it. If any bookies still talked to me. And I had a farm."

"Don't go stickin' yo' big red nose into this, Sherlock Holmes. Let the police —"

"Aw, what's one more dead circus act to the bulls? We kinkers take care of our own, don't we?"

Lotta looked sadly in the distance. "Used to."

"Don't tell me the rope wore through. Tillie just wasn't that careless. I'm gonna follow that rotten Rollo until he slips up. I'll be on him like a prowling panther. A black shadow. A lethal mist. But first —"

"First what?"

I held up my leg. "Can ya get my foot outta this bucket?"

☞

············ ◆ ············

James Finn Garner *wrote* **Politically Correct Bedtime Stories** *and the clown noir series starring Rex Koko. His eponymous website is named for him.*

JOE OESTERLE (JOEOPORTFOLIO.COM)

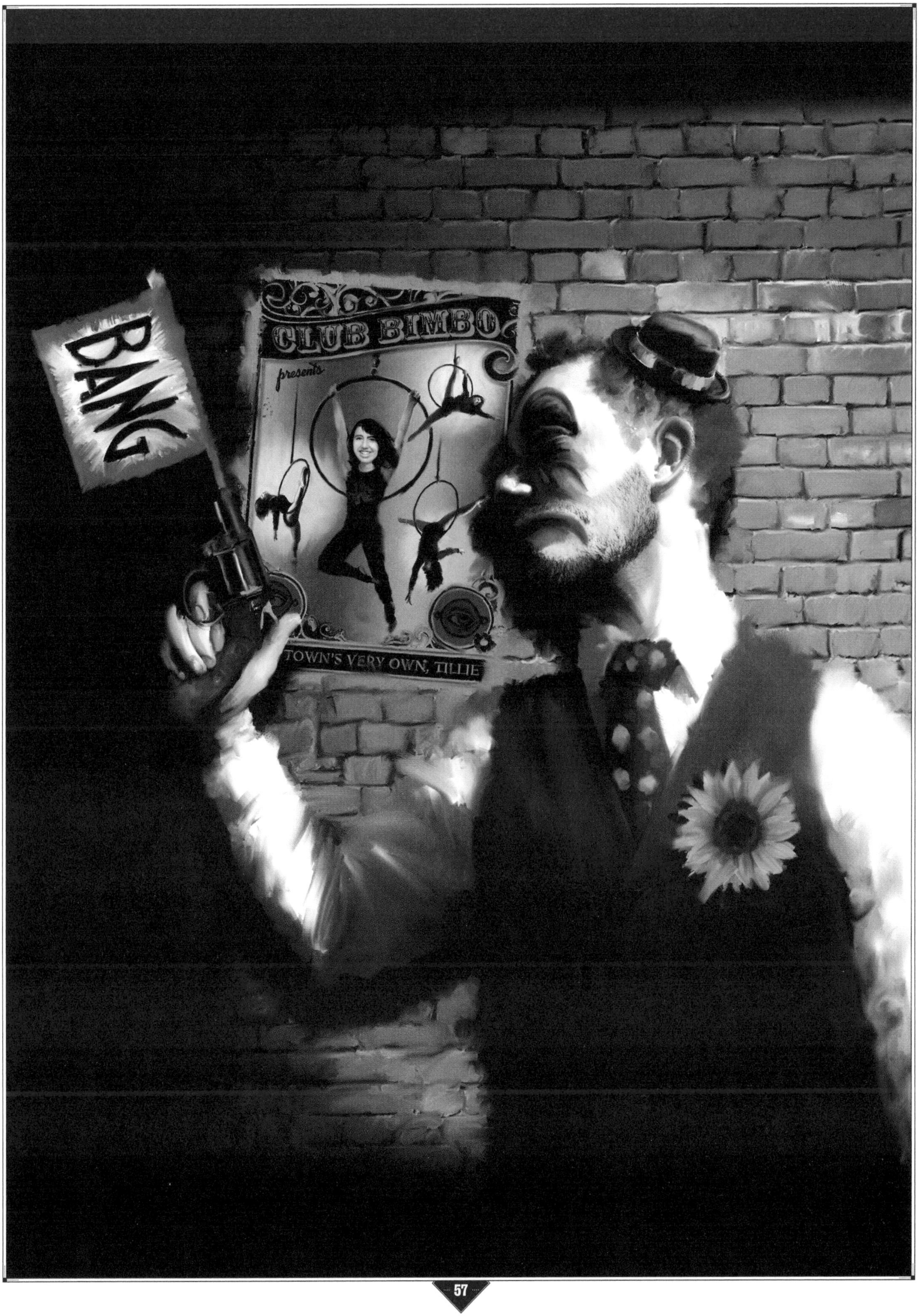
BANG
CLUB BIMBO
presents
TOWN'S VERY OWN, TILLIE

THE DYLAN THOMAS WORKOUT

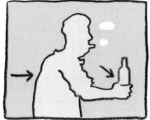  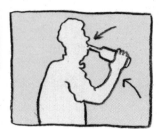 

KUPER

Evening was settling on Top Town, the time when we dust off our tricks and our popcorn and welcome the townies to our streets and alleys, the next best thing to a circus. The acrobats start limbering up, the fire-eaters begin roasting their molars, the blind pigs open their doors. And I was out there, trying to get answers and avoid setting off the mousetraps. I failed on both counts. Cheese wasn't any good, either.

Like so many itches in our part of town, this itch about Rollo showed no sign of going away. I staked him out by the Pie Car and tailed him through all the cooch shows on Griebling Street. He was walking around like the sixth Ringling Brother, without a care in the world. Rollo went from club to club, flirted with different dames—the widower showed no signs of grief, but that wasn't a crime. This was a trip for biscuits. All I had to show for the night was sore feet and sore fingers. And a pocketful of inedible cheese.

The next afternoon I brought a bottle of Coca-Cola over to share with Milt, who'd been running the side-show ever since Stick got hauled off to jail. Milt was good for an ear to the ground and a nose for hokum.

"Tillie used to drop in all the time," he said. "The most glamorous girl down here, and she came by on the regular, just to say hi to me and the freaks. Even took time with the ones who aren't all there." He tapped his spotted forehead with a bony finger and took a swig of soda.

I looked down his row of banners. Gordie the Dog-Faced Boy. Sailor Sam, the Sword-Swallowing Man."Electric"

Tessie Tesla. Only one person sat on the stage now.

"You mean, guys like Eddie Echo?" Eddie was sitting there on his stool as usual, same ill-fitting suit, same dumb look on his face, four hours 'til showtime. As his name implied, he was an astonishing mimic, able to imitate any audience member the instant they opened their yap.

Milt nodded. "The brains of a chicken, Eddie has, but Tillie would talk to him like he was Einstein."

"That bum Rollo didn't deserve her."

"Amen to that."

"Think it was an accident?"

He handed me back his empty Coke bottle. "Think you can get a diamond ring back on this?"

Around 5:00 I was at the Banana Peel, staring at my drink, not knowing what to do next. The other joeys were busy with a spit-take contest, doing it all wrong. "No, Slapsy, no," I coached, "if you want distance and volume, you've got . . ."

SPWISSSHHHH! I stood there dripping, and they all howled at me. Slapsy was actually pretty good, he just had a slight slice he needed to work on. A call came in on the blower, and Sid the Bartender said it was for me. Lotta was on the other end. "That Rollo has gone an' proposed to one of mah showgirls!"

"Which one? The lead in the French Revolution act?"

"Naw, Gloria, the one who plays Bathsheba in the big Old Testament number."

"'The Secrets of the Patriarchs'?" I smiled wolfishly. "Her act made me enroll in Bible study."

"Well, say a prayer, 'cause they're headed out of town tonight."

"Rollo can't lam outta here. He zotzed Tillie! I know he did!" Behind me, the spitting stopped.

"Gloria said the two of 'em are elopin' on the 7:30 train. Yew better come up with a plan, Mr. Detective, or they'll be gone with the wind!"

I hung up, then looked over at the silent, dripping men. "Joeys, I need your help." Thirteen heads are better than one, even if we were all a bunch of clowns.

Bingo owned a yellow, custom-built Model A that stood about waist high; it was the centerpiece of his act, but when he heard my plan, he gladly let us borrow the teeny jalopy. He even helped me paint "TAXI" across the door, which was a pretty long word to fit on that little thing. Then we went to the costume department and stole a jacket and a black cap that looked like a cabby's. I parked a block east of the Club Bimbo and waited for my chance.

Five minutes later, a weaving Rollo burst out of the front doors, dragging a flustered Gloria, stumbling on her heels. He looked around like it was in his contract that a car should be waiting for him. Rollo blew air from beneath his bottle-brush mustache and waggled his head in my direction. I revved up the engine, startled a couple pedestrians as I pulled out, and deposited my ersatz cab in front of him. It was all I could do to not run him over.

"Taxi, pally?" I asked, like I'd seen in the movies.

He gave me the stink eye when I came around to open the door. "Since when do they let clowns like you drive?"

"A joey's gotta eat," I said, grabbing the handle.

"Take us to the station," he commanded. Rollo moved to dive inside, but I pushed him back. "Hold on, sir, I gotta let out my other fare."

I held the door open, and Bingo walked out, giggling and squealing, "Thanks, Mr. 100% Real Cab Driver!"

Then Chiggers emerged with a salute. "That was the most authentic cab I ever done rode in!"

Then Happy Jingles, Goose, Pickles and 14 more joeys poured out of the back seat. Rollo's slow burn was one for the ages, as every clown of mine took his sweet time, tipping me imaginary quarters and falling over one another on the curb. Slinky brought up the rear, shouting "Dames ahoy!" as they all filed into the club.

Red-faced, the snake tried to climb in, when I stopped him again. "Hold on, sir," I said. "One last passenger."

Me, Rollo and Gloria watched the darkness in the back of the cab. Three seconds passed, four, five... then a female voice, high and strong, rang out: "How are you doing tonight?"

Rollo's face was ashen. His mouth opened, but no sound came out.

"Going somewhere, sweetheart?" the voice continued. "Not if I can help it. Not a chance."

I leaned into him. "What's the matter, pally? You don't look so good."

Rollo stuttered, "T...T...Tillie?"

"Let's have a little talk, just you and me, hmm?"

Rollo let out a scream and jerked back from the cab, tripping over the satchel behind him. Gloria looked confused, as usual.

I bent down, but instead of helping him up, I sneered in his ear, "Whaddaya expect, only two weeks in the ground?"

Rollo screamed, "Take her away!"

"You killed Tillie, didn't ya?" By now a crowd had gathered. "How'd you do it, Rollo? Did you gaff her line?"

The voice in the cab laughed so loudly, even I got a chill.

"Yes! Yes! I cut it through so it would break. I switched it."

"Where is it now?"

"I hid it. In the hay bales behind the Hippodrome! Just please! Take her away!"

"We'll take you away first." Lotta was standing in the door of the club. She grabbed Alvin the bouncer, and he didn't need any encouragement to hoist Rollo up and walkstep him away.

"Let's go find dat rope, Rollo, waddya say?" the bouncer growled as they left.

Chances were good they'd stop at a few other places around Top Town; before the night was through, Rollo would wish he were safe in the arms of the police.

The crowd thinned, leaving Gloria standing there, dumbfounded but still adorable. Finally she picked up her bag. "I guess I better get back to work and get out of these clothes."

I stuck my head into the cab to offer congratulations when Eddie Echo burst out, knocking me flat in his hurry. With a big loopy grin on his face, he shouted, "Dames Ahoy!" in a perfect imitation of Slinky, and strutted through the double doors. Chances were, he'd already forgotten his starring role in our charade.

I picked up Bingo's teeny car, leaned it against the wall in the alley, and put the steering wheel in my pocket. It was nice to have a plan of mine go right for a change. "No charge, Tillie," I said to the sky. "That fare was on the house." I joined the guys in the Bimbo. Lotta covered our drinks all night, even the spit-takes, something the old girl regrets to this day. **B**

ALL RIGHT, TIME FOR POSSE ROLL CALL!

IF YOU SIGNED UP FOR THE POSSE TO TRACK DOWN THOSE COWARDLY MURDERIN THIEVES, ARCHIE OVERKNOB, DICK GINGERFOP AND GRUNTS DINGLY, ANSWER WHEN I CALL YOUR NAME...

GRAVYBOAT JOHNSON!
AYE!

DUSTY CRINKLES!
AYE!

VERBLY FLABSON!
HERE!

BLINKY TICKS!
HERE!

BOBBY FARTKNIFED!
HERE!

CLOWSON FICKLESPATTER!
HERE!

LATHERS GREELY!
HERE!

FLIMSY ASSBUCKLER!
AYE!

DIRGE OBELISK
HERE!

SLIM HAMMERNUTS!
YO!

TRUMP: THE UNCANNY VALLEY OF BASIC HUMAN BEHAVIORS

BY JOE FOURNIER

TRUMP HAS A WAY OF TAKING THE SIMPLEST OF BEHAVIORS AND TURNING THEM INTO HIS OWN UNCANNY VALLEY OF OFF-PUTTING, HUMAN-LIKE PARODY.

SITTING

HONESTLY? ONLY THE LOWER HALF OF HIS BODY IS ACTUALLY SITTING. HAD HIS BUTT TOLD HIS UPPER TORSO, PERHAPS IT WOULDN'T BE HANGING OUT AND AWAY FROM THE CHAIR LIKE A CANTILEVER SLAB. WERE IT NOT FOR HIS LOAD-BEARING ELBOWS PLANTED ON HIS KNEES, THE WEIGHT OF HIS UPPER TORSO WOULD PROPEL HIM OUT OF THE CHAIR, ASS OVER TEACUP, AND SEND HIM ROLLING ACROSS THE ROOM.

WALKING

TRUMP'S WALK IS REALLY MORE OF A STALK. FROM THE WAIST DOWN, HE IS ALL LOCK-LEGGED, FRANKENSTEIN'S MONSTER WHILE, FROM THE WAIST UP, HE'S A DRINKING BIRD TOY FOREVER LOCKED IN HIS FORWARD LEANING, BEAK-WETTING CANT.

CROSSING HIS ARMS

WHEN TRUMP ATTEMPTS THIS TASK, HE LOOKS AS IF HE WERE WEARING AN INVISIBLE STRAITJACKET, OR A MAN TRYING TO SCRATCH HIS SHOULDER BLADES.

PRSRT STD
U.S. Postage Paid
Hanover, PA 17331
Permit No. 4

The American Bystander
1122 Sixth Street #403
Santa Monica, CA
90403

DRINKING

TO WATCH TRUMP TENTATIVELY SUCKLE ON A BOTTLE OF EVIAN WATER PUTS ONE IN MIND OF A GERBIL WORKING A SIPPER BOTTLE IN A CAGE.

BREATHING

"WHAT ABOUT INVOLUNTARY BEHAVIORS?" YOU ASK. "SURELY, HE CAN'T SCREW THOSE UP!" YOU'D THINK. BUT THIS SNIFFING, SNUFFLING, NOSE FLUTE OF A MAN WOULD PROVE YOU WRONG.

SMILING

SOME SMILES ARE ENDEARING, SOME ARE WELCOMING AND SOME ARE DOWNRIGHT WARMING WITH THE UNIQUE ABILITY TO REAFFIRM, TO EVEN THE MOST JADED AND CALLOUSED OF HEARTS, THAT THERE IS HOPE IN HUMANITY'S BETTER ANGELS.

AND THEN THERE ARE THOSE SMILES THAT YOU JUST WANT TO SLAP INTO NEXT WEEK!

SHAKING HANDS

HE **IS** CONSISTENT. WHETHER HE'S SHAKING HANDS WITH VIRILE, POWERFUL HEADS OF INDUSTRY, OR WITH WITHERED, INFIRMED OCTOGENARIANS, TRUMP SHAKES HANDS LIKE HE'S SAWING WOOD FOR WINTER, AND BY THE LOOKS OF IT, IT'S GONNA BE A LONG ONE!

Henry Phillips: The Later Years

As the saying goes, "It takes a visionary with a screw loose to transform the fastener industry!" Such a visionary was Henry Phillips.

With mass production taking over American manufacturing in the 1920s, the old slot-head screw was no longer sufficient. In the 1930s, Henry Phillips realized that a cross-head screw was the answer. The cross-head screw was self-centering, saving precious time on assembly lines. Also, something about torque or whatever. By 1940, Phillips' patented "Phillips head screw" had been widely accepted.

So what does a screw innovator do for a second act?

Henry Phillips spent years chasing further screw glory, becoming increasingly desperate and bitter as the failures piled up. Then, just when things seemed darkest, a surprise twist!

1946: The Moderne

Phillips's pitch: *"The insouciant tilt of one cross branch signals to cognoscenti that the screw business has entered an exciting new era of dynamic asymmetry! High style meets almost-as-good function in the Moderne, the must-have design for postwar industries hungry for the next big thing!"*

Phillips's "sophomore screw slump." Not produced.

1948: *Screwball!*

Phillips's lavish self-produced one-man Broadway show was billed as an evening of "fastener industry anecdotes, jokes, gossip and music." Ignored by critics and industry VIPs, the sparsely attended show closed after one awkward performance. Though extremely rare, the *Playbill* is not considered a collector's item.

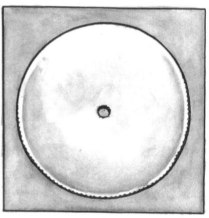

1949: The Unity

The pitch: *"The ultimate in understated screw spirituality! The radical design evokes the oneness of all creation and imbues modern manufacturing with the holiness craved by industry in these troubled times. Surrender to the Unity and welcome in a new era of fastener glory!"*

The product of Phillips's short-lived religious mania. The Unity's prospects were doomed by the fact that it couldn't be turned.

.... ◆ ....

Steve Young *is a veteran* **Letterman** *writer who's also written for* **The Simpsons.** *He is the main subject of the award-winning comedy music documentary* **Bathtubs Over Broadway.**

1951: The Comeback

The pitch: "That old Phillips magic is back as the master returns to his roots! Someone mention practicality? The Comeback has various slots, crosses, etc. that allow the screw to be turned, if desired. There's something for everyone in this updated classic screw head! Matching screwdriver projected to be available by 1957."

Embarrassed silence from the fastener industry.

1953: Screwtopia

In the summer of 1953, Phillips opened an elaborate amusement park in Anaheim, California. With attractions such as Screw Street USA, Threadland and Mr. Phillips's Wild Ride, Screwtopia was envisioned as "a rollicking, family-friendly screw-themed fantasy world" that would restore Phillips's fortune and professional reputation. Predictably, the public stayed away, and Screwtopia closed in September 1953. The land and facilities were purchased for pennies on the dollar by Walt Disney.

1955: Happy Screw

The pitch: "Too often, screw head design can veer into the soulless and antiseptic. Problem solved with Happy Screw! This heartwarming screw will boost assembly line morale and raise the spirits of the product end user. Smile — humanity and joy have come to the fastener business!"

As Phillips learned to his sorrow, there is no place for humanity or joy in the fastener business.

1956: Phillips for Him

In a desperate change of direction, Phillips launched a men's fragrance sold in a distinctive screw-shaped bottle, with "a musky tang of machine shop, old leather and lubricating oil." Although a failure at the time, unopened bottles of Phillips for Him now command modest prices among machine shop enthusiasts.

1958: The Screw You All

The pitch: *"Take it or leave it. I'm done. You people don't deserve me."*

With this conceptually bold, useless design, Phillips burned his remaining bridges with the fastener industry. However, in recent years, the Screw You All has been displayed by several small regional modern art museums.

1959: The Twist

Broke and depressed, Phillips nevertheless tried once more, devising a screw-themed dance and accompanying song. A friend with music industry connections noted some potential, and the song was recorded by Chubby Checker minus the Phillips head screw references. "The Twist" became one of the biggest hits in history. The fastener business was still out of reach, but suddenly Phillips was rich again.

Next time: Henry Phillips's ill-fated 1960s attempts to launch more hardware-themed dance crazes. **B**

A QUICK TOUR OF JOEY'S BIG-TIME MINI-GOLF

HOLE #1 MISTER FROG'S POND BRIDGE

DIFFICULTY: Easy-peasy!

HOLE #2 IKE THE GNOME'S WINDMILL

DIFFICULTY: Ike has let his property rot, so windmill no longer turns. Simple shot!

HOLE #3 REGULAR GOLF HOLE

DIFFICULTY: It's the big leagues! Try out a full-size course, and see how much you flail.

HOLE #4 WIZARD'S KEEP (Former scrap pile)

DIFFICULTY: You might need a spell to defeat this one! Or a tetanus shot.

HOLE #5 MEGA MAZE (cancelled)

WARNING SCORPIONS
MAZE ENTRANCE

DIFFICULTY: Maze was too complicated, so we filled with dirt. Skip to next one!

HOLE #6 GERALD'S BOG

DIFFICULTY: Unstable ground, miasmas, and a hole that sinks further into the bog every day.

HOLE #7 LOST TO THE SHADOWS

DIFFICULTY: Can't win this one, because we no longer know where the hole is!

HOLE #8 MOUNT GOLFUVIUS

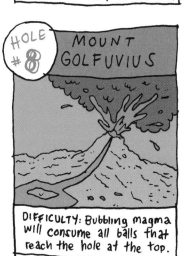

DIFFICULTY: Bubbling magma will consume all balls that reach the hole at the top.

HOLE #9 WHOLE HOLE

DIFFICULTY: You're in the hole now. You cannot leave the hole. How does it feel?

B

Prescription for Confusion

I went to fill a bunch of prescriptions for my wife after she had oral surgery. The woman at the counter asked my relationship to the person whose name was on the prescription. I said, "I'm her husband."

"So . . . spouse, then."

"Yes."

She clicked at her keyboard. "By marriage?"

I paused, first confused and then intrigued. I said, "What are my other options?"

The woman became slightly irritated. "It's a 'yes' or 'no' question, sir." She emphasized the word "sir," probably to make clear that she was being respectful although it sounded to me as though she doubted that "sir" was the right word, as though I had claimed a knighthood that had never actually been bestowed.

I said: "I'm sorry. Let's start again. I'm here to fill these prescriptions for my wife. I am her spousal husband."

The woman did not take her eyes from mine. She did not retype the information. "Yes. We've got that."

"Great."

She glanced at her monitor and then said, "By marriage?"

I knew my wife would still be numb from the Novocain for another two hours, so I felt no urgency in collecting the medications and rushing back to her. I decided to experiment. I said, "No."

The woman clicked something on her keyboard. Looked at the monitor. Clicked her keyboard again. She said, "It's not accepting that input."

"Okay. Then maybe try 'yes.'"

"Which is it?"

"Which is what?"

"Is it 'yes' or 'no'? You can't just give whatever answer you think is going to get you the drugs the fastest."

"I assure you, that's not what I was doing. My wife is, in fact, my spouse by marriage."

"You understand that Percocet is a Schedule II narcotic, sir?"

"Yes."

"You know there is an epidemic of opioid abuse in this country?"

I said, "Is knowledge of current events and trends in recreational drug use necessary to fill my wife's prescription?"

"A lot of people come in trying to score drugs."

"Do they come in with a prescription sheet that includes antibiotics and periodontal mouth wash?"

"I'm just trying to do my job."

"I can see that. I didn't mean to make it more difficult for you."

She glared at me, because she could apparently hear at least some of the things I was deliberately not saying. She said, "I'm going to need to get the pharmacist."

"I assumed you were a pharmacist."

"Do I look like a pharmacist to you, sir?"

I looked at her white lab coat. I looked at the picture ID clipped to her pocket. I said: "My mistake. I was confused by the pharmacist costume and the apparent ability to sell me Schedule II narcotics."

"So you *are* aware that Percocet is a Schedule II narcotic!" Her tone implied that she had caught me out, Perry Mason-style, with her clever, roundabout method of getting to the truth.

She walked away, and another young woman came to the counter. She also wore a white lab coat with a picture ID clipped to the pocket. "Hi! I understand you're having some difficulty?"

"Just trying to fill a prescription for my wife," I said.

She looked over the prescription and looked at my driver's license. She said, "No problem at all, sir." She implied nothing with the use of the word "sir" so I felt pretty good about how this round was going. "And you understand that Percocet is a Schedule II Narcotic?"

I said, "Do I look like a pharmacist?"

She looked at me, possibly checking for lab coats and name tags. "I'm just informing you. Percocet is a Schedule II Narcotic."

"Good to know."

"We're currently experiencing an epidemic in opioid abuse."

"The other woman mentioned it. Yes."

"Yes. Louise."

I said, "Okay. I mistook her for a pharmacist."

She said: "Oh, good heavens no! Does she look like a pharmacist to you?"

"I might have fallen for a stereotype."

"So, we have to ask you a few questions before we can release this prescription."

"Okay."

"You are not the patient. That would be your wife. Yes?"

I said, "Yes."

"So… " she scanned the monitor for a moment and then said: "Oh. Okay. So that's 'spouse.'" She clicked a key. "And that would be by marriage. Is that correct?"

I sighed and said: "Yes. My wife is my spouse by marriage."

"Very good, then," she clicked something on the keyboard. Then she said, "I don't understand why people do that to themselves," as she typed my driver's license number into a field on the computer.

"Get married?"

"No. The opioid use. I don't understand what happens in people's lives that makes them want to be stoned all the time."

I said, "I think I'm starting to understand it."

"That's what my husband says when I talk about it."

"Your spouse?"

"Yes."

"By marriage?"

"Oh, yes! Absolutely by marriage!" She said it with such joyous certainty that I could not help but believe that marriage was the best possible way to be related to one's spousal husband. B

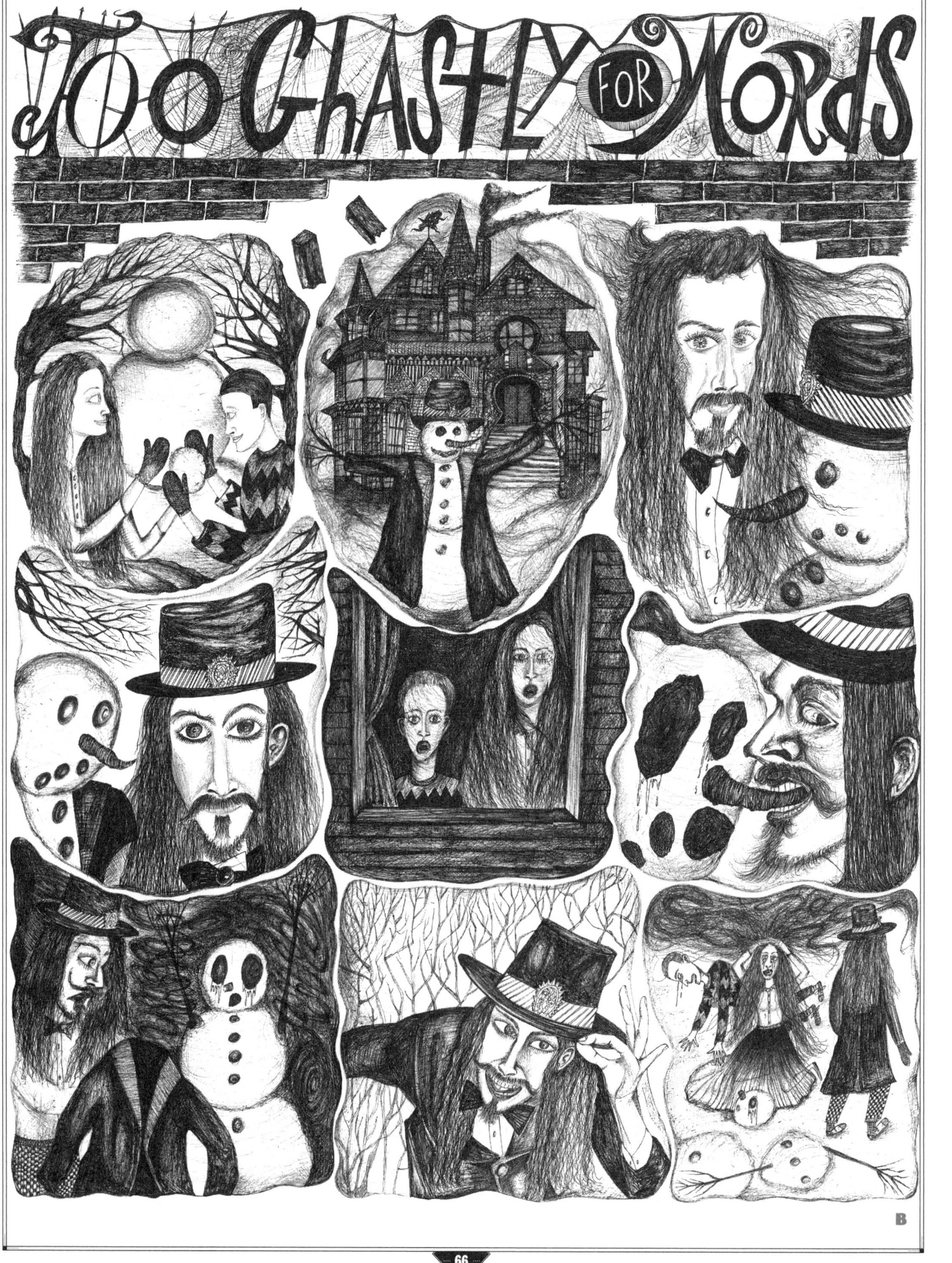
TOO GHASTLY FOR WORDS

MORT GERBERG
ON THE SCENE
A 50-Year Cartoon Chronicle

Mort Gerberg's social-justice-minded—and bitingly funny—cartoons have appeared in magazines such as *The Realist*, *The New Yorker*, *Playboy*, and the *Saturday Evening Post*. And as a reporter, he's sketched historic scenes like the fiery Women's Marches of the '60s and the infamous '68 Democratic National Convention. Fantagraphics Underground is proud to present a 50-year career retrospective of this vital cartoonist, collecting his magazine cartoons, sketchbook drawings, and on-the-scene reportage sketches in one handsome volume.

LETTER FROM MELANIA

First, you will hear from my lawyers. Then—night will descend. • By Emily Flake

To the Editors *of* The Daily Telegraph:

With regard to the insulting and defamatory article written about myself by that Nina Burleigh woman, I was pleased to read the retraction and apology that my human lawyers wrested from you. This, in addition to the financial penalty we shall exact, fulfills your obligations as written in the laws of man.

Now, however, it is time to speak of the other laws.

I have enjoyed your groveling and your money. But the laws of which I speak are older, and cannot be appeased by apologies, no matter how public and self-abasing. Your gift of money is only useful in that it pleases me to know how deeply it hurts your institution to give so much. There are much more interesting punishments to come.

Let us address the falsehoods committed by the one called Nina Burleigh. She claimed that I met Donald in 1996, when in fact I only allowed him into my physical orbit in 1998 (this came, of course, after decades of preparation of his spirit on a metaphysical plane, of which the human woman knows nothing. Ha! Ha! Imagine if she knew all that happens there! She would never

EMILY FLAKE is FLOTUS Whisperer for *The American Bystander*.

sleep for trying to claw such knowledge from her skull!). She claims that Donald helped with my modeling career. In truth, he had nothing to do with it—the modeling was an amusing but inevitable side effect of the illusory body I chose for my human form. Men see this flesh-casing and wish to take its picture, intent upon pleasuring themselves to it at a later time. They cannot imagine my true form, which would cause their members to crawl deep inside their bodies, and in any case, cannot be photographed. The picture-taking amused me, particularly the time I let my human mask slip just a bit, and that photographer's hair went completely white. Existence on this plane is often dull, and a woman must be allowed her hobbies.

If this were all there was, I would be satisfied with having blinded the writer and editors in question. However, there is the matter of my father. The insect Burleigh writes that my father was a fearsome presence who ran my family with an iron fist. That she spoke only of the puppet-body Viktor Knavs and not of my true Monstrous Source is no matter—when the Name of the Father is invoked, there are consequences. I'm afraid this goes a little beyond a standard blood debt.

Perhaps you are familiar with the dream in which you think you are awake, but you cannot move or speak? Do you know this sense of panic and dislocation? Can you now imagine that feeling amplified many thousands of times? Then imagine you are being stripped of your skin, *but on the inside*. Now add the feeling of a celebrity you adore retweeting something you wrote, but only to call you "an asshole." All this begins to approximate what it feels like to have your living soul burned slowly away by a vengeance spell. Which is what is in store for you, whenever I get around to it.

While I long to see the flayed yet living bodies of your staff and freelancers dance in the wind above Fleet Street, the time for such spectacle is yet to come. For now, I content myself with the Words I have B-rr-n chanting in his quarters, the effects of which will be felt, for now, only by your etheric selves. Suffice it to say I look forward to a future in which you exercise much more caution in what you commit to print—though I have a difficult time imagining you'll be able to use words for any other purpose than to beg your puny God for annihilation.

I look forward to the swift resolution of this matter and the timely dissolution of your very beings. *May the Source be Ever Appeased!*

Thoughts & Prayers,
Melania

WHAT AM I DOING HERE?

Intrepid traveler travels to Iceland and finds...not much • By Mike Reiss

As luck would have it, the absolute best vantage point to see the Northern Lights is this cabin in the middle of nowhere.

Iceland Left Me Cold

It's one of the few facts we all remember from grade school: "Greenland is actually icy, and Iceland is really green!" And like everything we learned in school, it's completely wrong. Thanks to climate change, Greenland is getting greener by the day. And Iceland is cold as crap. It's chilly in the summer and in the winter, only an idiot would go there.

I am that idiot.

My wife dragged me to Reykjavik in February to see the Northern Lights. We checked into a hotel that featured prime viewing of the phenomenon. Every forty minutes, from 2 to 8 in the morning, hotel workers would bang on our door shouting. "They're happening! They're happening!" We'd run out into the polar night, still in our pajamas, only to hear "You missed it! You missed it!"

We did catch a couple of good looks at the aurora borealis, and let me say something no one else has the courage to admit: They're a big, celestial nothin'. They look great in *National Geographic* because, by some cruel joke of a sadistic God, the Northern Lights photograph beautifully. To my naked eye, they were wispy clouds of gray-green smoke; through my camera lens, I saw an electrical fireworks spectacular.

The Northern Lights: gorgeous on camera, zilch in person. Just like Julianne Moore.

Luckily, there's so much more to see in Iceland. Actually, just three things.

There's Blue Lagoon, a huge spa warmed by geothermal energy and tourist pee. Each year, 700,000 visitors (twice the population of Iceland!) come to soak in God's Jacuzzi. And since the waters are said to have healing powers, many, many of those tourists suffer from skin diseases like eczema. This is Iceland's No. 1 attraction: a bubbling slow cooker jammed with the population of Albuquerque, lots of them blistered, flaking and oozing. I'd sooner share a toothbrush with Willie Nelson.

Iceland's most photographed site is Hallgrimur's Church, which sounds like a setting from *The Lord of the Rings*. (Indeed, Peter Jackson scouted locations here that he duplicated in his fifty-seven-hour film trilogy: caves of ice, impossibly sharp peaks, frozen waterfalls, and squat, shaggy horses that resemble comedy writer Bruce Vilanch.) The church is Iceland's tallest and largest, and is said to look like Superman's Fortress of Solitude, or two packages of string cheese leaning up against each other.

But to me it was a stylized pair of praying hands, soaring hundreds of feet in the air, a stunning tribute to the power of faith and God's love.

And, it's walking distance to the penis museum!

Yes, not far from the cathedral is the Icelandic Phallological Museum, a single tiny space crammed with hundreds of penises (again, like Bruce Vilanch). Twenty whale peckers cross overhead like rafters, while several more run from floor to ceiling; these are load-bearing wieners. My wife seemed particularly taken with a tanned walrus wang, which jutted out of the wall like an obscene water main. Feeling threatened, I kept trying to steer her towards a display of hamster penes, but she wasn't budging.

We still hadn't given up on the Northern Lights. My wife rented a cabin deep in the heart of Iceland that was said to be ideal for night sky viewing. As we drove out of Reykjavik, we stopped at what should be a tourist spot, but isn't: the lone, unremarkable grave of Bobby Fischer. He'd been the greatest chess player who ever lived; then he went a little nutso, spent a dozen years as a fugitive, had all his fillings removed, and did some jail time in Japan. This

MIKE REISS is Intrepid Traveler for *The American Bystander*.

world-famous Jewish kid from Brooklyn wound up in a small suburb of Reykjavik, buried in front of a tiny church that actually looks like a church. It was a surprising final move in the unorthodox endgame of Bobby Fischer.

We arrived at our cabin, which was miles from anything else in Iceland, which itself is miles from anything on earth. The owner was Dag, a Kenny Loggins-looking hippie who seemed unaware that being a hippie was no longer a thing. His previous houseguest had been Queen guitarist Brian May, who'd also come to see the aurora borealis. (Mr. May, like many rock musicians, has a doctorate in astrophysics.)

Dag served us a hearty stew of his own recipe, then led us outside to see the Northern Lights. There were none—the sky was as thickly clouded as it's ever been in human history. That's when Dag went a little nutso—he wandered into an icy lake up to his waist and tried to catch us some fish with his bare hands. Illuminated by the headlights of his Jeep, I realized how much Kenny Loggins resembled Charles Manson.

We returned to Dag's home empty-handed. We were a hundred miles from the nearest living soul, trapped in a cabin with a crazed, wet hippie. Our vacation had turned into a horror movie, and not a particularly good one. I was certain we'd wind up ingredients in the hearty stew Dag served his next guests.

The next morning rose bright and cloudy. Dag woke up chipper and full of hippie hope, determined to show us a good time. He set each of us on his prized snowmobiles and gave us the forty seconds' training needed to master them. Snowmobiles may look exciting, but they get boring fast; they're basically golf carts that drive on snow. Only an idiot couldn't handle one.

I was that idiot.

I immediately got stuck in a patch of wet snow and started gunning the engine to escape. The snowmobile belched black smoke...then burst into flame.

"What did you...how did you...it's not possible!" Dag sputtered. In a country full of surreal sights, this was the most Daliesque: a mellow hippie completely losing his cool while a snowmobile blazed like a yule log.

Who needs the Northern Lights? **B**

P.S. MUELLER THINKS LIKE THIS

The cartoonist/broadcaster/writer is always walking around, looking at stuff • By P.S. Mueller

My Way

And now, my hand is here
Looks like my face, but I'm uncertain
That hand, I keep it near
Just in case my mushroom's hurtin'
I've grabbed a life that's stacked
I've combed it each and every which way
And worse, much worse than this
I wrecked it my way
Egrets, I've had a few
But in a stew I dare not mention
I hid what I hid from you
And deducted that exemption
I sold each quarter horse
As primo steaks along the highway
And worse, much worse than this
I wrecked it my way
Yes, there were crimes, I'm sure you knew
When I stuffed in more than you could chew
But if I may, where there is clout
A strangled nation cannot shout
I grabbed it all, took Putin's call
And wrecked it my wayyyyyyyyyyyyyyy

Suppertown

I had only been a pastry manager for a few months at the I-80 Suppertown when Carleen was hired on as a full time server. All the servers were cute in their little Quaker outfits. I was used to that.

P.S. MUELLER is Staff Liar of *The American Bystander*.

But Carleen dressed like a Quaker lady after she was off the clock, something I have to confess more or less sort of kind of got to me in a certain way, if you know what I mean. She had me from "Thee."

At first I thought Carleen was only after meringue. It is true that I was easily beguiled by her special way of walking sideways through a room, and it is equally true that she had no trouble accepting my weekly offering of a heady hatbox full of freshly cooked meringue. I have no idea what she did with all that sticky stuff and have never asked, which is probably also why she agreed to be my wife.

Suppertown was on its way to becoming a wonder of the world when Carleen and I first got together. "All you can eat" had replaced "E. Pluribus Unum" years earlier during a restless period of consolidation, experimentation, and merciless competition. We had become a restaurant where whole families checked in for a week or more, where every booth had a private bathroom, where "customers" became "residents." By the time we reached middle age, the decision was made to lease the entire interstate middle strip and put wheels under Suppertown.

Carleen and I did well at Suppertown. Her days of delivering cheddar bombs to the angries in Booth 11 were long gone and I had moved up the chain to become the location manager. *TIME* named us as the 2036 "Supper Couple of the Year." I'm sad to say Carleen traded in her Quaker outfit for proper business attire once I no longer had unlimited access to meringue. I don't ask about it.

Not long after the first of the giant diesel Suppertowns began rolling in 2040, we retired to accept the company's offer of life-long Suppertown accommodations and transfers. I never eat the pastry and Carleen steers clear of the cheddar bombs. We have been sitting idle at a train crossing for the past three hours, glumly waiting for a Dinner Train to pass, when Carleen returns from the bathroom wearing a Quaker Lady Bonnet and whispers "Go find some meringue and meet me in our stateroom."

Ten Reasons Why That Guy Is Dead To Me

He took more than his share of the money and then the fucker rolled on us. He's dead to his own sister, too.

That other guy had something, some tiny, nearly imperceptible sway over the Academy of Motion Picture Arts and Sciences. He dropped a couple of comments in some Hollywood bar, and the next thing you knew, Dances With fucking Wolves took Best picture. He knows who he is and he is five-star dead to me.

That guy! Over there crouching behind the greeting cards. He's crazy as boneless space monkeys and thinks he's my parole officer. He would be dead to me if he wasn't alive.

The guy who broke into my house and cooked and ate my Rottweiler right in my own kitchen is dead to me and the dog.

Twice at work this kid who looks like a pinched fuse on Lightning Day used the word Kafkaesque in my presence. I will have him persecuted, but he is already dead to me.

I live a double life, which is hard to do with people like Phil around all the time. Phil is dead to me.

The guy who sold me a bunch of bad grappling hooks is dead to me.

Many years ago a withered fortune teller told me you would show up straight from the knuckle farm and punch me in the face. When you're done you will be dead to me.

That other guy from college, the nerdy one with the pet oyster. He glanced over his should at me with snide contempt and eventually came to own the "7" button on your phone. He's dead to me on general principles.

Oh yeah, and the whaler. I mean why in the great realm of all fuck would a guy hunt and kill whales? And he's a hobbyist! Dead to me, I swear.

Salt Water Daffy

There are things in the ocean that you shouldn't oughta see.
There are things in the ocean that just shouldn't oughta be.

Argonaut bones and a lotta rotten sailors rattle after battle on the seabed floor.
There's U-boats too, and Japanese whalers.

And all the bottom-feeders there are screaming for more.

Amelia's plane and unlucky sacks of puppies,
stewin' in the blue and very briny briny deep,
make a main course meal for a school of passing guppies
or a grouper in stupor who is going back to sleep.

There are things in the ocean that you shouldn't oughta see.
There are things in the ocean that just shouldn't oughta be.

Jellyfish think about as well as they are able,
swellin' up and tellin' other jellyfish their plan.
The man' ray swims to an offer on the table
for a taste of phony leather from a sunken minivan.

Anemones wave at a passing piece of freighter,
busted up and rustin' by the Marianna trench.
There's a tater fish somewhere waitin' for a tater
and a big snail hopin' for a cruiser full of French.

There are things in the ocean that you shouldn't oughta see.
There are things in the ocean that just shouldn't oughta be. B

MUELLER

TEXAS STYLE? AGAIN?

ROSS MACDONALD *(@brightworkillo) has contributed cartoons and humor to many fine periodicals, written four children's books, and created props for your favorite movie or TV show.*